Unit structure

1.0 Objectives

After studying this unit, you should be able to understand:
- The **Meaning** of Managerial Economics.
- The **Nature** and **Characteristics** of Managerial Economics**.**
- The **Scope** of Managerial Economics**.**
- The **Relationship** of Managerial Economics with other branches of knowledge.

1.1 Introduction

Managerial Economics is indeed an off-shoot of the Second World War. Before the outbreak of this war, the study of economics was purely an academic exercise, while business was a pure practice based on common practical sense of human mind. The Second World War created a tremendous pressure on scarce economic resources of the world. Thus, the need for optimum utilization of resources intensified further, which ultimately gave birth to a new discipline popularly known as Managerial Economics.

The present business world has become very dynamic, complex, uncertain and risky. Therefore taking appropriate, correct and timely decision has become a challenging and tedious task. The existence/ survival and growth of business basically depends on such decisions. Undoubtedly, Managerial Economics is a friend. philosopher and guide to the business leaders and managers. Further, the growing complexity of decision-making process, the increasing use of economic logic, concepts, theories and tools of economic analysis in the process of decision-making and rapid increase in the demand for professionally trained managerial man power increased the importance of the study of managerial economics as a separate discipline of managerial curriculum. In this unit, we would be studying the meaning, nature and scope of Managerial Economics and its relationship with other branches of knowledge.

1.2 Meaning and Definition of Managerial Economics

The terms '**Managerial Economics**' and '**Business Economics**' are often synonyms and used interchangeably in managerial studies. It is also known as '**Economics for Managers**'. Basically, Managerial Economics is an **Applied Economics** in the sphere of business management. It is an application of economic theory and methodology[1] to decision-making problems faced by the business firms. Thus, it is the economics of business or managerial decisions or it is the process of application of principles, concepts and techniques and tools of economics to solve the managerial problems of business organizations. Some important **definitions of Managerial Economics** are given below :

"Managerial Economics is economics applied in decision-making. It is a special branch of economics bridging the gap between the economic theory and managerial practice. Its stress is on the use of the tools of economic analysis in clarifying problems in organizing and evaluating information and in comparing alternative courses of action."   **-W. W. Haynes**

"Managerial Economics is the integration of economic theory with business practice for the purpose of facilitating decision-making and forward planning by management."

- Spencer & Siegelman

"The purpose of Managerial Economics is to show how economic analysis can be used in formulating business policies."   **-Joel Dean**

By analyzing the various definitions of managerial economics given above, we come to the conclusion that managerial economics is the study of economic theories, logic, concepts and tools of economic analysis that are used in the process of business decision-making by the business managers in taking rational, correct and timely decisions. Managerial Economics is that part of economic theory which, in general, is concerned with business activities and in particular, concerned with providing solutions to problems arising in decision-making of business organizations. Indeed, it is **an integration of economic theory and business practices**. Therefore, Managerial economics lies on the borderline of Economics and Business Management act as complementarity and bridge between Economics and Management. From this point of view, managerial economics is that branch of knowledge in which the concepts, methods and tools of economic analysis are used for analyzing and solving the practical managerial problems with the purpose of formulating rational and appropriate business policies. **Basically managerial economics concentrates on decision process, decision models and decision variables.** This can be explained by the following **schematic chart**:

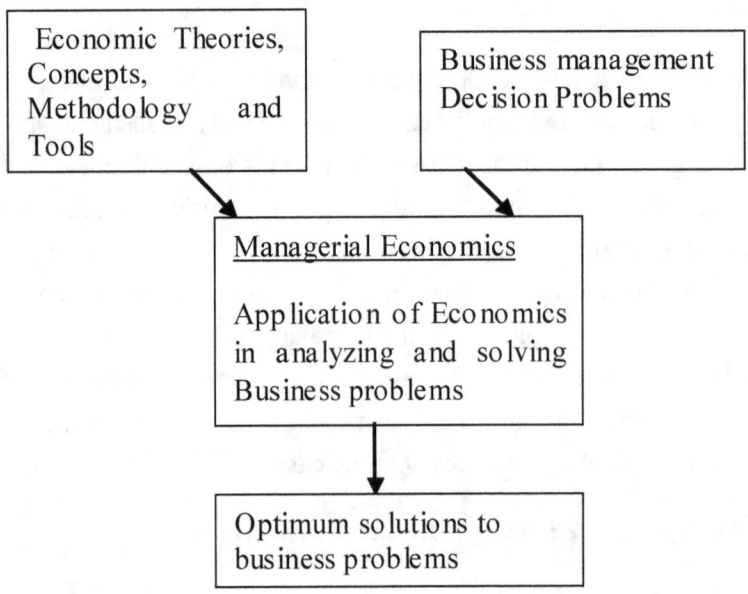

1.3 Characteristics of Managerial Economics

Prof. D .M .Mithani has mentioned the following broad salient features of Managerial Economics as a specialized discipline:

- It involves an application of Economic theory – especially, micro economic analysis to practical problem solving in real business life. It is essentially applied micro economics.

- It is a science as well as art facilitating better managerial discipline. It explores and enhances economic mindfulness and awareness of business problems and managerial decisions.

- It is concerned with firm's behaviour in optimum allocation of resources. It provides tools to help in identifying the best course among the alternatives and competing activities in any productive sector whether private or public.

For the sake of clear understanding of the nature and subject matter of managerial economics, the point-wise analysis of **main characteristics** of managerial economics is given below:

- **Micro economic analysis**: The main part of the study of managerial economics is the behaviour of business firm/s, which is micro economic unit. Therefore, managerial economics is essentially a micro economic analysis. Under the study of managerial economics, the problems of firm are analyzed and solved through the application of economic methods and tools. It does not study the whole economy.

- **Economics of the firm:** According to **Norman F. Dufty,** Managerial Economics includes, that portion of "Economics known as the theory of firm, a body of the theory which can be of considerable assistance to the businessman in his decision-making". For instance, the study of managerial economics includes the study of the cost and revenue analysis, price and output determination, profit planning, demand analysis and demand forecasting of a firm. As already stated earlier, the another name of managerial economics is 'Economics of the Firm.'

- **Acceptance of use & utility of macro economic variables:** In understanding the overall economic environment of an economy and its influence on a particular firm, the study and knowledge of macro economic variables or macro economics is a must. For example, the study of Monetary, Fiscal, Industrial, Labor and Employment and EXIM policy, National Income, Inflation etc. is done in managerial economics as to know the influences of these on the business of a firm. The study of macro economic variables helps in understanding the influence of exogenous factors on business activities of a firm. Without the study of important macro economic variables, **proper environmental scanning** is not possible.

- **Normative approach:** Managerial Economics is basically concerned with value judgment, which focusses on 'what ought to be'. It is **determinative rather than descriptive** in its approach as it examines any decision of a firm from the point of view of its good and bad impact on it. It means that a firm takes only those decisions which are favourable to it and avoids those which are unfavourable to it. The emphasis is on '**Prescriptive**' models rather than on '**Descriptive**' models.

- **Emphasis on case study:** In place of purely theoretical and academic exercise, managerial economics lays more emphasis on case study method. Hence, it is a practical and useful discipline for a business firm. It diagnises and solves the business problems. Therefore, it **serves as lamp post of knowledge** and guidance to business professionals / organizations in arriving at optimum solutions.

- **Sophisticated and developing discipline:** Managerial Economics is more refined and sophisticated discipline as compared to Economics because it **uses modern scientific methods of statistics and mathematics**. Not only this, the **methods of Operational Research** and Computers are also used in it for building scientific and practical models for analyzing and solving the real business problems under uncertain and risky environment.

- **Applied/Business Economics:** Managerial Economics is an application of economics into business practices and decision-making process; therefore, it is an applied economics/business economics. **The concepts of economic theory that are widely used in managerial economics are the following**:

  - Demand and Elasticity of demand
  - Demand forecasting
  - Production Theory
  - Cost Analysis
  - Revenue Analysis
  - Price determination under different market conditions/structures
  - Pricing methods in actual practice
  - Break-even analysis
  - Linear Programing
  - Game Theory
  - Product and Project Planning
  - Capital Budgeting and Management
  - Criteria for public investment decisions

  Basic concepts of Managerial Economics/Economic concepts applied to business analysis

  - Marginalism / Marginal Principle
  - Incrementalism / Incremental Principle
  - Equi-Marginalism /Equi- Marginal Principle
  - Discounting Principle
  - Opportunity Cost principle
  - Risk and uncertainty
  - Profits
  - Firm, Industry and Market
  - Economic and Econometric Models

- **Study of business environment:** Business environment in present world has not only become more complex, but also more dynamic. In a very complex and rapidly changing environment, making correct and timely decisions is a tedious task. Managerial Economics helps in understanding the business environment of firm/s.

1.4 Nature of Managerial Economics

Generally, it is believed that Managerial Economics is a blend of science and art because on one hand, it is a systematic study of economic concepts, principles, methods & tools, which are used in business decision-making process and on the other hand, it is the study of how these are used and applied in best possible manner in analyzing and solving business problems. In fact, science is a knowledge acquiring discipline, whereas arts is a knowledge applying discipline.

The following basic questions arise about the nature of Managerial Economics:
1. Whether managerial economics is a science or an art or both; and
2. If it is a science- then it is a positive science or a normative science or both

We would examine these issues systematically one by one in the coming paragraphs.

Managerial Economics is **both knowledge acquiring and knowledge applying** discipline. Thus, it can be concluded that managerial economics is **science and arts both**.

The best method of doing a work is an art and managerial economics is also an art as it helps us in choosing the best alternative from among the many available alternatives. Not only this, it also implement best alternative with best possible method.

After knowing the answer of first question, we would examine whether the managerial economics is a positive science or a normative science or a blend of both. Before knowing the answer of this question, we should understand the meaning of positive and normative science.

Positive Science is a systematic knowledge of a particular subject wherein we study the **cause and effect** of an event. In other words, it explains the phenomenon as: **What is, what was and what will be**. Under the study of positive science, principles are formulated and they are tested on the yardstick of truth. Forecasts are made on the basis of them. From this point of view, **managerial economics is also a positive science as it has its own principles/theories/laws by which cause and effect analysis** of business events/activities is done, forecasts are made and their validities are also examined. For instance, on the basis of various methods of forecasting, demand forecasts of a product is made in managerial economics and the element of truth in forecast is also examined/tested.

Normative Science studies things as they ought to be. Ethics, for example, is a normative science. The focus of study is **'What should be'**. In other words, it involves value judgment or good and bad aspects of an event. Therefore, normative science is **perspective** rather than **descriptive**. It cannot not be neutral between ends.

Managerial economics is also a **normative science** as it suggests the best course of an action after comparing pros and cons of various alternatives available to a firm. It also helps in formulating business policies after considering all positives and negatives, all good and bad and all favours and a disfavours. Besides conceptual/theoretical study of business problems, practical useful solutions are also found. For instance, if a firm wants to raise 10% price of its product, it will examine the consequences of it before raising its price. The hike in price will be made only after ascertaining that 10% rise in price will not have any adverse impact on the sale of the firm.

On the basis of the above arguments and facts, it can be said that managerial economics is a **blending of positive science with normative science**. It is positive when it is confined to statements about causes and effects and to functional relationships of economic variables. It is normative when it involves norms and standards, mixing them with cause and effect analysis. Managerial economics is **not only a tool making, but also a tool using science**. It not only studies facts of an economic problem, but also suggests its optimum solution.

Business ethics forms the core of managerial economics as cultural values, social customs and religious sentiments of the people coin the normative aspect of business activities. These things matter in designing production pattern and planning of the business in a country/area. For instance, a modern multi-national corporation has to consider the socio-cultural and religious moods / sentiments of the people before launching its product. The main purpose is not to hurt the sentiments of the people but to promote the well-being of the people along with business. Thus, we can **conclude** by saying:

- **Managerial economics is a science as well as an art.**

- **Managerial economics a positive and normative science both.**

- **Being of the determinative/perspective nature, the focus is on what should be or business decisions are based an value judgment considering the beneficial and harmful aspects of such decisions.**

1.5 Scope of Manegerial Economics

Economics has two major branches namely Microeconomics and Macroeconomics and both are applied to business analysis and decision-making directly or indirectly. Managerial economics comprises all those economic concepts, theories, and tools of analysis which can be used to analyze the business environment and to find solutions to practical business problems. In other words, managerial economics is **applied economics**

The areas of business issues to which economic theories can be applied may be broadly divided into the following two categories:

- Operational or Internal issues; and
- Environmental or External issues

Micro Economics Applied to Operational Issues

Operational problems are of **internal nature**. They arise within the business organization and fall within the perview and control of the management. Some of the important ones are:

- Choice of business and nature of product, i.e., what to produce;
- Choice of the size of the firm, i.e., how much to produce;
- Choice of technology, i.e., choosing the factor combination;
- Choice of price, i.e. ,how to price the commodity;
- How to promote sales, i.e., sales promotion measures;
- How to face price competition;
- How to decide on new investment;
- How to manage profit and capital;
- How to manage inventory, i.e., stock of both finished goods and raw material

The above mentioned issues fall within the ambit of micro economics, therefore, the following constitute the scope of managerial economics:

Theory of demand

- Consumer behaviour- maximization of satisfaction
- Utility analysis
- Indifference curve analysis
- Demand analysis and elasticity of demand
- Demand forecasting and its techniques/methods

Theory of production and production decisions

- Production function [Inputs and output relationship] in short-run and long-run
- Cost and output relationship in short-run and long-run
- Economies and diseconomies of scale

- Optimum size of firm and determining the size of firm.
- Deployment of resources [labor and capital] for having optimum combination of factors of production.

Analysis of market structure and pricing theory

- Determination of price under different market conditions
- Price discrimination
- Multiple pricing policy
- Advertising in competitive markets
- Different pricing policies and practices

Profit analysis and profit management

- Nature and types of profit
- Profit planning and policies
- Different theories of profit

Theory of capital and investment decisions

- Cost of capital and return on capital-choice of investment projects
- Assessing the efficiency of capital
- Most efficient allocation of capital
- Capital budgeting

Macro Economics Applied to Business Environment

Environmental issues relate to general environment in which business operates. They are related to overall economic, social and political environment of the country. The following are the **main ingredients of economic environment** of a country :

- The type of economic system- capitalist, socialist or mixed economic system.
- General trends in production, employment, income, prices, saving and investment.
- Volume, composition and direction of foreign trade.
- Structure of and trends in the working of financial institutions- Banks, NBFCs, insurance companies an other financial institutions.
- Trends in labour and capital market.
- Economic policies of the government- Fiscal policy, Monetary policy, EXIM- policy, Industrial policy, Price policy etc.
- Social factors- value system, property rights, customs and habits.
- Social organizations- Trade unions, consumer unions and consumer co-operatives and producers unions.
- Political environment is constituted of the following factors:
- Political system-democratic, socialist, communist, authoritarian or any other type.
- State's attitude towards private sector
- Policy, role and working of public sector
- Political stability.
- The degree of openness of the economy and the influence of MNCs on domestic markets- Integrations of nation's economy with rest of the world (Policy of globalization)

The environmental factors have a far reaching influence on the functioning and performance of firm/s. Therefore, business managers have to consider the changing economic, social and political environment before taking any decision. Managerial economics is however, **concerned with only the economic environment and in particular with those which form the business climate.** The study of social and political factors falls out of the perview of managerial economics. It should, however, be borne in mind that economic, social and political factors are inter-dependent and interactive.

The environmental issues mentioned above fall within fourwalls of macro economics, therefore the following constitute the scope of managerial economics:

Issues related to Macro Variables

- General trends in economic activities of the country
- Investment climate
- Trends in output
- Trends in price - level (state of inflation)
- Consumption level and its pattern
- Profitability in business expansion

Issues related to Foreign Trade

- Trade relation with other countries
- Sector and firms dealing in exports and imports
- Exchange rate fluctuations
- Inflow and outflow of capital
- Trends in international trade- volume, composition, and direction
- Trends in international prices of various goods and services
- International monetary mechanism
- Rules, regulations and policies of WTO

Issues related to Government Policies

- Regulation and control of economic activities of private sector business enterprises
- Enforcing the government rules and regulations for imposing of social responsibility
- Striking balance between firm's objective of profit maximization and society's interest
- Policy and regulatory measure for reducing social costs in terms of environmental pollution, congestion and slums in cities, basic amenities of life such as means of transportation and communication, water, electricity supply etc.

1.6 Relationship of Managerial Economics with Other Disciplines

By its nature, managerial economics borrows heavily from several other disciplines. The nature and scope of managerial economics can also be understood well by studying its relationship with other disciplines. Managerial economics draws heavily from the following disciplines:

Economics and Econometrics – As stated earlier that managerial economics is an application of economic theory into business practices / management. Managerial economics **uses both micro and macro economics**-their concepts, theories, tools and techniques. In managerial economics, we also use various types of models such **as schematic models** (diagrams) **analog models** (flow charts) and **mathematical models and stochastic models**. The roots of most of these models lie in economic logic. Economics also tells us the art of constructing models. **Empirically estimated functions**, which are being used in managerial economics are basically econometric estimates.

Mathematics and Statistics – Mathematical tools are widely used in model building for exploring the relationship between related economic variables. Most of the decision models are constructed in terms of mathematical symbols. Geometry, trignometry and algebra are different branches of mathematics and they provide various tools & concepts such as logarithms, exponentials, vectors, determinants, matrix algebra, and calculus, differentials and integral.

Similarly, statistical tools are a great aid in business decision-making. Statistical tools such as theory of probability, forecasting techniques, index numbers and regression analysis are used in predicting the future course of economic events and probable outcome of business decisions. Statistical techniques are used in collecting, processing & analyzing business data, and in testing the validity of economic laws.

Operational Research (OR) – OR is used for solving the problems of allocation, transportation, inventory building, waiting line etc.. **Linear programming** and **goal programming models** are very useful for managerial decisions. These are widely used OR techniques. In fact, OR is an **inter-disciplinary solution finding technique**. It combines economics, mathematics and statistics to build models for solving specific problems and to find a quantitative solution there by.

Accountancy – It provides **business data support** for decision-making. The data on costs, revenues, inventories, receivables and profits is provided by the accountancy. Cost accounting, ratio analysis, break-even analysis are the subject matters of accountancy and they are of great help to managers in decision-making.

Psychology and Organisation Behaviour (OB)–In fact, managerial economics analyses the individual behaviour of a buyer and seller [microeconomic units]. Psychology is helpful in understanding the behavioural aspects like attitude and motivation of individual decision making unit. **Psychological Economics**-a new discipline of recent origin analyses the buyer's behaviour useful for marketing management. **Behavioural models** of firms have also been developed based on organization psychology and micro economics to explain the economic behaviour of a firm.

Management Theory – Management theories bring out the behaviour of the firm in its efforts to achieve some predetermined objectives. With change in environment and circumstances, both the objectives of firm and managerial behaviour change. Therefore sufficient knowledge of management theory is essential to the decision-makers. The basic knowledge of the **principles of personnel, marketing, financial** and **production management** is required for accomplishing the task.

1.7 Summary

It is now universally accepted that the Managerial Economics has emerged as a separate branch of knowledge in management studies. Managerial Economics is the study of economic theory, logic and tools of economic analysis that are used in the process of business decision making. Economic theories and techniques of economic analysis are applied to analyze business problems, evaluate business options and opportunities with a view to arriving at an appropriate business decision. Infact, it is an applied economics. The important features of Managerial Economics are: Micro economic nature, economics of the firm, use of macro economic variables, normative nature, focus on case study method, applied use of economics and more refined and developing discipline.

The scope of managerial economics spreads both to micro and macro economics. The theory of demand, theory of production, analysis of market structure and pricing theory, profit analysis and management, theory of capital and investment decisions are the subject matter of micro economics.

Macro economic issues pertain to macro economic variables, foreign trade and various policies of the government. Operational issues are internal and they are part of micro economics, while environmental issues are exogeneous and they are part of macro economics. Both these together constitute the subject matter and scope of managerial economics.

Managerial economics is a science as well an art. It is basically a normative science involving value judgment. It is a tool making as well as tool using discipline. The most important disciplines on which managerial economics draws heavily are Economics and Econometrics, Mathematics and Statistics, Operational Research, Accountancy, Psychology & Organizational Behaviour and Management.

1.8 Key Words

- **Managerial Economics :** is an applied Economics in the field of business management. It is an application of economic theory and methodology in the business decision-making process. It is an integration of economic theory with business practices.

- **Micro Economics:** It is that branch of Economics in which the study of an individual economic unit is done. For instance, the study of a firm is a subject matter of micro economics. It is also known as the method of slicing.

- **Macro Economic:** It is that branch of Economics in which the economy as a whole is studied. It is also known as the economics of lumping / aggregation.

- **Macro Economic Variables :** These are the variables which relate to the entire economy of a nation / globe such as National Income, Inflation, Recession and they constitute the part of overall economic environment.

- **Positive Science:** It pertains to the cause and effect relationship of an event. It is a factual analysis, therefore, it studies 'What is".

- **Normative Science:** A science which studies "What ought to be". In other words, it involves value judgement, hence it is perspective in nature.

1.9 Self Assessment Test

1.   What does economic theory contribute to Managerial Economics?

2.   What is the contribution of psychology and organization behavior to Managerial Economics?

3.   How is mathematics & statistics and operational research useful to Managerial Economics?

4.   List the important characteristics of Managerial Economics.

5.   Summarize the scope of Managerial Economics as a learner.

6.   Why should you study the Managerial Economics?

1.10 Suggested Books / References

1.   Mithani D.M. : Managerial Economics, Himalaya Publishing House, Mumbai

2.   Dwivedi, D.N. : Managerial Economics, Vikas Publishing House Pvt. Ltd, New Delhi

3.   Misra & Puri : Economics for Managers, Himalaya Publishing House, Mumbai

4.   Adhikary M. : Managerial Economics, Khosla Educational Publishers, Delhi

5.   Mathur N.D., : Managerial Economics, Shivam Book House Private Limited, Jaipur

2 Theory of Demand

Unit Structure

2.0 Objectives

After studying this unit, you should be able to:

- Appreciate the significance of demand analysis
- Understand the concepts of demand and types of demand
- Know the factors influencing the demand for a product
- Distinguish between the changes in quantity demanded and changes in demand
- Understand the demand schedule, demand curve and the law of demand.

2.1 Introduction

Without understanding the concept of demand and supply, economic analysis is incomplete and meaningless. Demand is one of the most important economic decision variables. The analysis of demand for a firm's product plays a crucial role in business decision-making. Demand determines the size and pattern of market. All business activities are mostly demand driven. For instance, the inducement to investment and production is limited by the size of the market of products. The profit of a firm is influenced and determined by the demand and supply conditions of its output and inputs. Even if a firm pursues other objectives than the profit maximization, demand concepts are still relevant. For instance, the objective of firm is 'customer service' or discharging 'social responsibility'. Without analyzing the needs of customers and evaluating social preferences, these objectives cannot be achieved. All these variables are an integral part of the concept of demand. Thus, the **demand is the mother of all economic activities**. The firm's production planning, sales and profit targeting, revenue maximization, pricing policies, inventory management, advertisement and marketing strategy all are dependent on the demand of its product. Not only this, the survival and growth of a firm also depends on the demand for its product. In this unit, we shall be examining various concepts of demand and the law of demand.

2.2 Concepts of Demand

Demand is a technical economic concept. It is a different and broader concept than the 'desire' and "want". The following **five elements are inclusive** in it:

1. Desire to acquire a product-willingness to have it,
2. Ability to pay for it-purchasing power to buy it,
3. Willingness to spend on it,
4. Given/particular price, and
5. Given/particular time period.

The presence of **first three elements constitute the 'want'**. Thus, it is evident that **without reference to specific price and time period, demand has no meaning**. For instance, Ram is desirous of buying a car, but he does not have sufficient money to buy it, it can't be termed demand as he does not have sufficient purchasing power to buy a car. Suppose, Ram is has sufficient money to buy a car, but he does not want to spend on it-even in such a situation, the desire of Ram for a car will remain a desire. What is required for being a demand is sufficient purchasing power and willingness to spend on that product for which he has desire to acquire. Not only this, the demand for a product must be expressed in reference to certain given price and time period, otherwise it won't be a demand. Thus, the **concept of demand has following characteristics**:

1. It is effective desire / want,
2. It is related with certain price, and
3. It is related with specific time period.

According to **Benham**, "The demand for any thing at a given price is that amount of it, which will be bought at a time at that price." The complete definition of demand has been given by **Prof. Meyers** According to him, "The demand for a good is a schedule of the amount that buyers would be willing to purchase at all possible prices at any one instant of time."

Distinct concepts of demand

1. **Direct and derived demand:** Direct demand refers to the **demand for goods meant for final consumption**. It is the **demand for consumer goods** such as sugar, milk, tea, food items etc. On the contrary to it, derived demand refers to the **demand for those goods which are needed for further production** of a particular good. For instance, the demand for cotton for producing cotton textiles is a case of derived demand. Indeed, **derived demand is the demand for producer's goods;** i.e., the demand for raw materials, intermediate goods and machine tools and equipment. The another example of derived demand is the **demand for factors of production**. The derived demand for inputs also depends upon the degree of substitutability/complementarities between inputs used in production process. For example, the degree of substitutability between gas and coal for fertilizer production.

2. **Domestic and industrial demand:** The distinction between domestic and industrial demand is very important from the pricing and distribution point of view of a product. For instance, the price of water, electricity, coal etc. is deliberately kept low for domestic use as compared to their price for industrial use.

3. **Perishable and durable goods demand:** Perishable goods are also known as **non-durable / single use goods**, while durable goods are also known as **non- perishable/ repeated use goods**. Bread, butter, ice-cream etc are the fine example of perishable goods, while mobiles and bikes are the good examples of durable goods. **Both 'consumers' and 'producers' goods may be of perishable and non-perishable nature**. Perishable goods are used for meeting immediate demand, while durable goods are meant for current as well as future demand. Durable goods demand is

influenced by the replacement of old products and expansion of stock. Such demand fluctuates with business conditions, speculation and price expectations. **Real wealth effect** has strong influence on demand for consumers durables.

4. **New and replacement demand:** New demand is meant for **an addition to stock**, while replacement demand is meant for **maintaining the old stock of capital**/asset intact. The demand for spare parts of a machine is a good example of replacement demand, but the demand for new models of a particular item [say computer or machine] is a fine example of new demand. Generally, **new demand is of an autonomous type**, while the **replacement demand is induced** one-induced by the quantity and quality of existing stock. However, such distinction is more of a degree than of kind.

5. **Final and intermediate demand:** The demand for semi-finished goods and raw materials is derived and induced demand as it is dependent on the demand for final goods. The demand for final goods is a direct demand. This type of distinction is based on types of goods- final or intermediate and is often employed in the context of **input-output models**.

6. **Short run and long run demand:** The distinction between these two types of demand is made with specific reference to time element. Short- run demand **is immediate demand** based on available taste and technology, products improvement and promotional measures and such other factors. **Price-income fluctuations** are more relevant in case of short- run demand, while changes in **consumption pattern, urbanization and work culture** etc. do have significant influence on long –run demand. Generally, long-run demand is for future consumption.

7. **Autonomous and induced demand:** The **demand for complementary goods** such as bread and butter, pen and ink, tea, sugar milk illustrate the case of induced demand. In case of induced demand, the demand for a product is dependent on the demand/purchase of some main product. For instance, the demand for sugar is induced by the demand for tea. Autonomous demand for a product is **totally independent of the use of other product**, which is rarely found in the present world of dependence. These days we all consume bundles of commodities. Even then, all direct demands may be loosely called autonomous. The following equation illustrates the determinants of demand.

$$D_X = á + â\ P_X$$

Here á is a symbol of autonomous part - which captures the influence of all non-price factors on demand, whereas $âP_X$ symbolizes the induced part-D_X is induced by P_X, given the size of β.

8. **Individual and Market Demand:** The demand of an individual for a product over a period of time is called as an individual demand, whereas the sum total of demand for a product by all individuals in a market is known as market/collective demand. This can be illustrated with the help of the following table:

Individual and Market Demand Schedule

Price of Commodity (Rs.)	Units of X Commodity Purchased by			Market (Total)
	A	B	C	
6	5	10	12	27
7	4	8	9	21
8	3	5	7	15

The distinction between individual and market demand is very useful for personalized service/target group planning as a part of sales strategy formulation.

9. **Total market and segmented market demand:** A market for a product may have **different segments based on location, age, sex, income, nationality etc**. The demand for a product in a **particular market segment** is called as segmented market demand. Total market demand is a **sum total of demand in all segments of a market** of that particular product. Segmented market demand takes care of different patterns of buying behaviour and consumer preferences in different segments of the market. Each market segment may differ with respect to delivery prices, net profit margins, element of competition, seasonal pattern and cyclical sensitivity. When these differences are glaring, demand analysis is done segment-wise, and accordingly, different marketing strategies are followed for different segments. For instance, airlines charge different fares from different passengers based on their class-economy class and executive/business class.

10. **Company and industry demand:** A company is a **single firm** engaged in the production of a particular product, while an industry is the **aggregate / group of firms** engaged in the production of the same product. Thus, the company's demand is similar to an individual demand, whereas the industry's demand is similar to the total demand. For instance, the demand for iron and steel produced by Bokaro plant is an example of company's demand, but the demand for iron and steel produced by all iron and steel companies including the Bokaro plant is the example of industry demand. **The determinants of a company's demand may be different from industry's demand**. There may be the inter-company differences with regard to technology, product quality, financial position, market share & leadership and competitiveness. The understanding and knowledge of the relation between company and industry demand is of great significance in understanding the different market structures/forms based on nature and degree of competition. For example, under perfect competition, a firm's demand curve is parallel to ox-axis, while under monopoly and monopolistic competition, it is downward sloping to the right.

2.3 The Law of Demand

The law of demand states **an inverse relationship between the price of a commodity and its quantity demanded**, if other things remaining constant (Ceteris Paribus), i.e., at higher price, less quantity is demanded and at lower price, larger quantity is demanded.

Prof. Paul Samuelson has lucidly defined the law of demand. According to him, "if a greater quantity of a good is thrown on the market then - other things being equal- it can be sold only at a lower price."

Assumptions of the law of demand: The law of demand is based on the following important ceteris paribus assumptions:

- The money income of consumer should remain the same.
- There should be no change in the scale of preference (taste, habit & fashion) of the consumer.
- There should be no change in the price of substitute goods.
- There should be no expectation of price changes of the commodity in near future.
- The commodity under question should not be prestigious or of snob appeal.

Reasons behind downward sloping demand curves

As we know that most of the demand curves slope downward to the right because of an inverse relationship between the price of a commodity and its quantity demanded. But the question is why inverse relationship exists between the price and quantity demanded. Economists have mentioned the following reasons of this relationship:

1. **Application of the law of diminishing marginal utility:** The marginal utility curve slopes downward, hence the demand curve also slopes downward to the right.

2. **Substitution effect:** The commodity under question becomes cheaper with fall in its price in comparison to its substitutes, therefore demand increases.

3. **Income effect:** With fall in price of the commodity, demand increases due to increase in **real income** as a result of **positive income effect**.

4. **Falling prices attract new consumers** as the commodity now becomes affordable to them.

5. With fall in price of the commodity consumers start using it in less important uses, therefore demand increases. Generally, commodities have different / varied uses.

Exception to the law of demand or upward sloping Demand curve

Sometimes, the law of demand may not hold true, although rarely. In such a situation, a consumer may purchase **more at higher price and less at lower price**. In this unusual condition, demand curve will be upward sloping from left to the right as shown below:

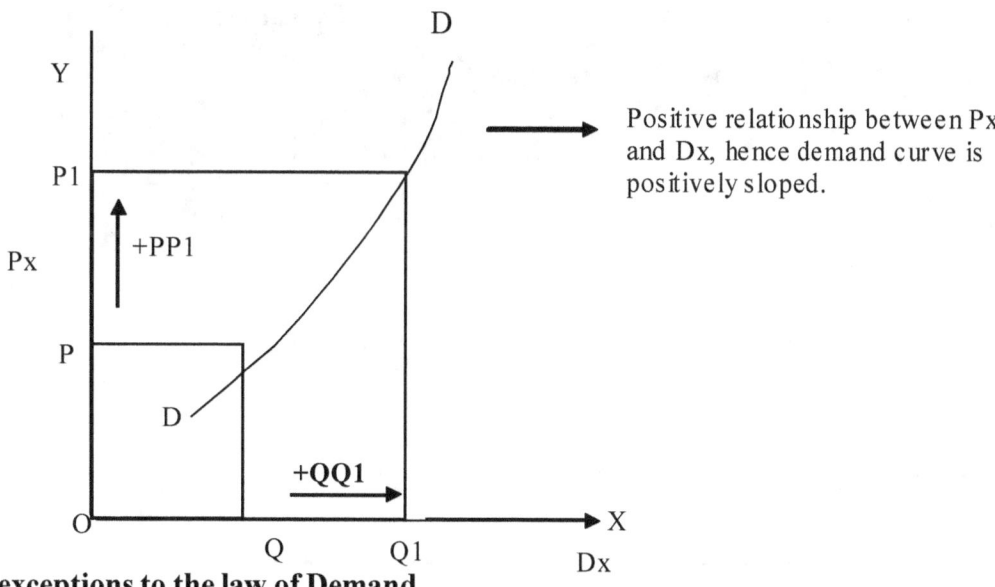

Positive relationship between Px and Dx, hence demand curve is positively sloped.

few real exceptions to the law of Demand

1. **Giffen goods:** In case of such goods, the income effect is negative and it is stronger than positive substitution effect. Examples of such goods are coarse grain like jowar, bajra and coarse cloth.

2. **Articles of Distinction/Snob appeal:** They satisfy aristocratic desire to preserve exclusiveness for unique goods- such goods are purchased only by few highly rich people for snob appeal. For instance, very costly diamonds, rare paintings, Rolls-Royce- cars and antique items. These goods are called "**veblen goods**" after the name of an American economist.

3. **Consumers psychological bias or illusion** about the quality of commodity with price change. They feel that high priced goods are better quality goods and low price goods are inferior goods.

Prof. Benham has given an example of a **book of photographs** during the first world war. The sale of second edition of the book increased tremendously inspite of rise in its price, though the book contained the same photographs without any change.

4. The law of demand does not apply in case of **life saving essential goods** and also **in times of extraordinary circumstances** like inflation, deflation, war and other natural calamities. The law also does not hold true in case of **speculative demand**. Stock markets are the fine examples of speculative demand

2.4 Demand Schedule and Demand Curve

Demand schedule is a **statistical/tabular statement** showing the different quantities of a commodity which will be bought at its different prices during a specified time period. It is a table which represents functional relationship between price of a commodity and its quantity demanded. Demand schedule can be **for an individual** –known as **Individual Demand Schedule (IDS)** and it can be for the **whole market**-known **as Market Demand Schedule(MDS)**.MDS can be obtained by aggregating the IDS as illustrated earlier in this unit under the heading of individual and market demand.

Demand Curve: By plotting the demand schedule on graph, we can obtain the demand curve. According to **Prof. Samuelson**, "Picturization of demand schedule is called the demand curve". Accordingly, there can be two types of demand curve- **Individual Demand Curve based on IDS** and **Market Demand Curve based on MDS**.

Demand curve may be linear as well as non-linear depending upon the nature of demand function.

Linear Demand curve

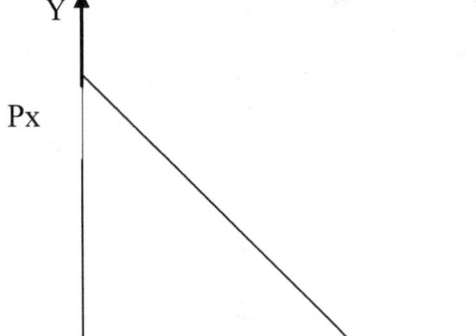

Non-Linear Demand Curve

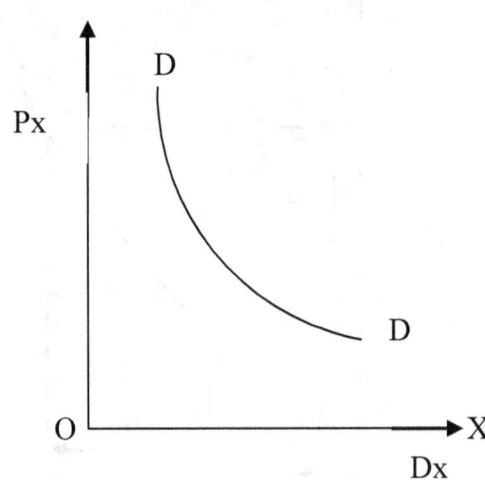

2.5   Determinants of Demand / Demand Function

The demand for a particular commodity is influenced by so many factors- they together are known as determinants of demand in technical jargon, it is stated as demand function. A demand function in mathematical terms expresses the **functional relationship between the demand for a product and its various determining factors.** For instance,

$$D_x = f(Px, Ps, Pc, Yd, T, A, W, C, E, P, G, U)$$

Here:

Dx   =   Demand for x commodity (say, tea)

Px	=	Price of x commodity (of tea)
Ps	=	Price of substitute of x commodity (coffee)
Pc	=	Price of complementary goods of x commodity (sugar, milk)
Yd	=	Disposable income of the consumer
T	=	Taste and Preference of the consumer
A	=	Advertisement of x commodity
W	=	Wealth of purchaser
C	=	Climate
E	=	Price expectation of the consumer
P	=	Population
G	=	Govt. policies pertaining to taxes and subsidies
U	=	Other factors (unspecified/unidentified)

Under normal circumstances, the **impact of these determinants** can be explained as under:

1. Demand for x is inversely related to its own price. As price increases, the demand tends to fall and vice-versa

$$\frac{\delta Dx}{\delta Px} < 0 \qquad \text{This is price- demand relation, depicting the } \textbf{price- effect} \text{ on demand}$$

2. Disposable income (budget) of the consumer is one of the important variables to influence the demand. With increase in income, people buy more of superior/normal goods and less of inferior / Giffen goods. The **income effect** on demand may be **positive as well as negative**.

$$\frac{\delta Dx}{\delta Yd} \begin{matrix} > 0 \\ < \end{matrix} \qquad \text{This is an income – demand relation, depicting } \textbf{income effect.}$$

The **Bandwagon** effect or **Demonstration effect** may influence the demand and it is a result of **relative income.**

3. The demand for x is also influenced by the prices of its related goods (substitutes or complements as the case may be). **Substitution effect is always positive** and **complementarity effect is negative** as stated earlier

$$\frac{\delta Dx}{\delta Ps} > 0, \qquad \frac{\delta Dx}{\delta Pc} < 0 \qquad \text{This is cross-demand relation showing the } \textbf{substitution and complementary effect}$$

4. The demand for x may be sensitive to price expectation of the consumer (depends on psychology of the consumer)

$$\frac{\delta Dx}{\delta E} \begin{matrix} > 0 \\ < \end{matrix} \qquad \textbf{Price expectation} \text{ effect on demand is not certain. For instance, } \textbf{Speculative demand.}$$

5. Accumulated savings and expected future income, its discounted value along with present income – permanent and transitory - all together constitute the nominal wealth of a person. We may also

add to his current assets and other forms of physical capital adjusted to price level – This is **real wealth** and it has influence on the demand. For example, a person has a two wheeler, now may demand a four wheeler and it can be stated as

$$\frac{Dx}{\delta w} > O$$

6. Taste, preference and habits of consumers may also have decisive influence an the pattern of demand. Social customs, traditions and conventions are **Socio – psychological** determinants of demand – these are **non-economic and non-market factors**.

7. Advertisement has great influence on demand. It is in observed fact that sales turnover of firms increases up to a point due to advertisement – this is **promotional effect** on demand and can be stated as

$$\frac{\delta Dx}{\delta A} \begin{array}{c} > \\ < \end{array} O$$

8. Climate also influences the demand for different goods. For instance, the demand for coolers and A.C. increases in summers, while their demand declines in winters.

9. The number and composition (age, sex etc.) of population also influence the demand for goods.

10. Government policy on taxes and subsidies also influences the demand of different goods differently. For instance, increase in tax rates / imposition of new taxes reduce the demand, while increase in subsidies increase the demand.

2.6 Types of Demand

Prof. Baber has mentioned the following three types of demand based on three important factors [price of commodity, income of the consumer and prices of related goods] influencing the demand:

1. **Price demand:** This type of demand indicates the '**price effect**', which explains the impact of changes in price of a particular product on its quantity demanded, if other factors influencing the demand remaining constant. The functional relationship between price of a product and its quantity demanded can be put in the following equation form and be illustrated with price demand schedule:

$$D_X = f[P_X]$$

Here: D_X = Demand for x commodity, f = functional relation, and Px = Price of x commodity

Price Demand Schedule

Price of X Commodity (Px) (Rs.)	Demand for X Commodity (Dx) (units)	Particulars
2	100	Inverse relationship between
3	80	Px and Dx showing negative
4	40	price effect.

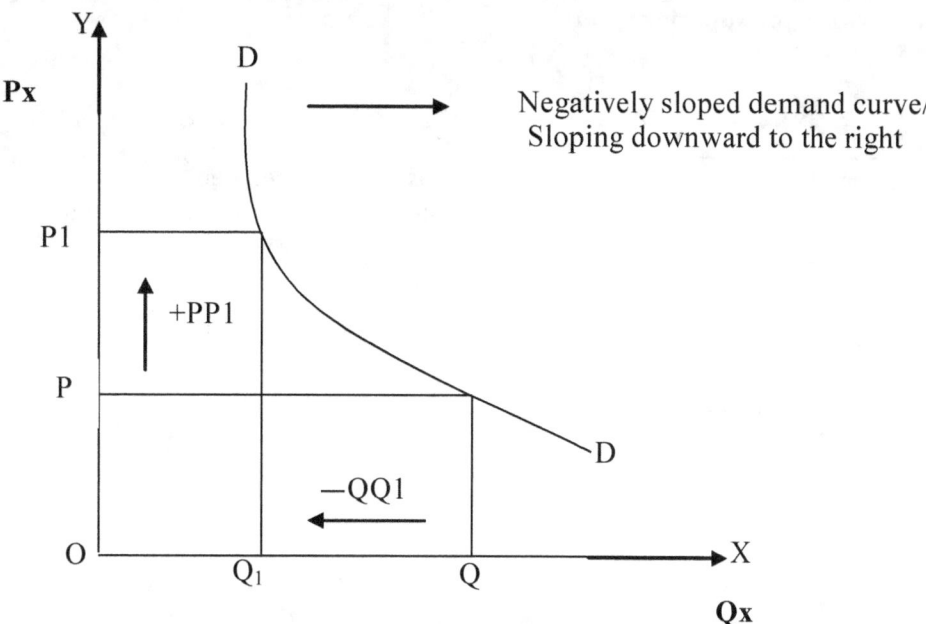

2. **Income demand:** This type of demand shows the '**income effect**,' which explains the impact of changes in the income of the consumer on the demand for a particular product, other things remaining constant. The functional relationship between the income of the consumer and the demand for a product can be put as under:

$$D_x = f[y]$$

Here: Dx = Demand for x commodity,

f = Functional relation, and

Y = Income of the consumer.

From income demand point of view, goods can be **classified into two categories** as explained under:

a) **Superior goods:** In case of such goods **income effect is positive** as demand for them increases with increase in income of the consumer and vice-versa. This is illustrated in the following table:

Income of the consumer(Y) (Rs.)	Demand for x commodity (Dx) (units)	Particulars
1000	10	Positive relationship between Y & Dx showing positive income effect
2000	20	
3000	30	

b) **Inferior goods:** The demand for such goods declines with increase in the income of the consumer and vice-versa. The **income effect is negative** in case of such goods. Since this was observed, for the first time, by **Robert Giffen**, hence to give him honour, inferior goods are termed as **Giffen goods**. But there is difference between inferior goods and Giffen goods. Only those inferior goods are termed as Giffen goods, on which a consumer spends comparatively a large part of his income. Thus, all **Giffen goods are inferior goods, but all inferior goods are not Giffen goods**. The example of Giffen goods is coarse grain and coarse cloth and this is illustrated in the following table:

Income of the consumer(Y) (Rs.)	Demand for x Commodity (Dx) (units)	Particulars
1000	10	Inverse relationship between Y & Dx depicting negative income effect
2000	05	
3000	02	

19

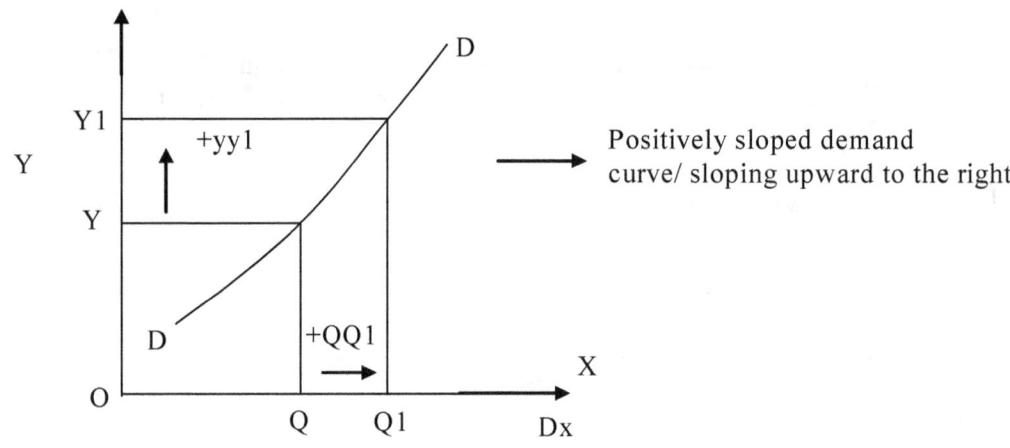

Demand curve for superior goods

Positively sloped demand curve/ sloping upward to the right

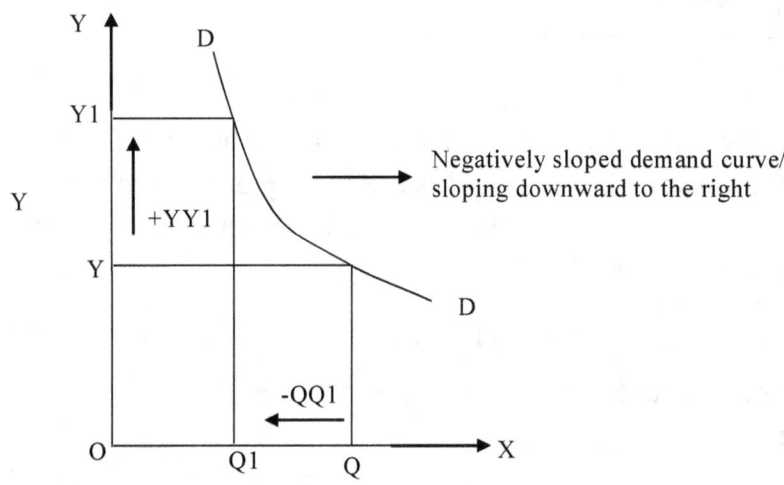

Negatively sloped demand curve/ sloping downward to the right

3. **Cross demand:** The demand for a commodity Dx is also influenced by the changes in price of its related goods (substitutes or complementary goods as the case may be). This is technically termed as '**cross effect**' and can be put in the following equation:

$$D_X = f\,(pr) \qquad or \qquad D_X = f\,(\,py\,)$$

Here: D_X = Demand for x commodity, f = function, and Pr = Price of related goods,
Py = Price of Y commodity- related to x either as substitute or complementary good.

The cross demand of a commodity **depends on the nature of its related goods** –from this point of view, it can be of the following **two types**:

(a) **Cross demand for substitutes:** Substitute goods / competing goods can easily be used in place of each other for satisfying a particular want. For example, tea and coffee or pepsi and coca-cola or wheat and rice etc. The impact of changes in price of Y commodity (Py) on the demand for X commodity (D_X) is called '**Substitution effect**',which is **always positive** as illustrated in the following table:

Price of coffee (Py) (Rs.)	Demand for tea (Dx) (cups)	Particulars
8	1000	Direct relationship between
9	1200	Py & D_X showing positive
10	1800	Substitution effect

20

(b) **Cross demand for complementary goods:** Those goods which are used together for satisfying a particular want are known as complementary goods. For instance, tea, sugar and milk or pen and ink etc. The **complementary effect is negative** as the price of one good increases, the demand for other good decreases and vice-versa. This is illustrated in the table given below:

Price of car (py) (Lakh Rs.)	Demand for petrol (Dx) (Litres)	Particulars
2	10,000	Inverse relationship
3	8,000	between Py & Dx indicating
4	4,000	negative complementary effect

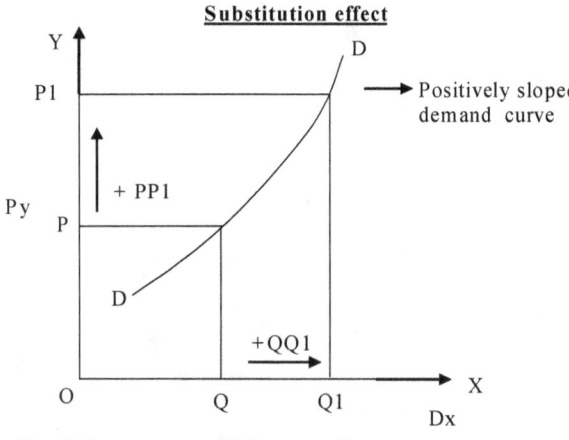

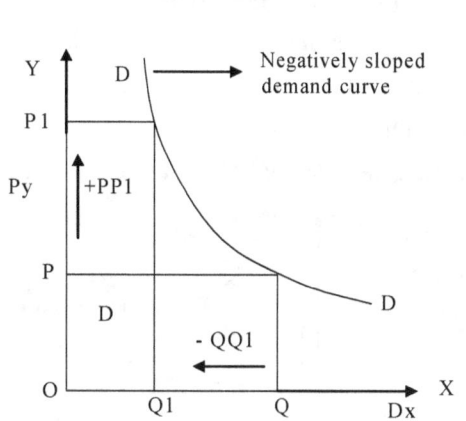

3. Other types of demand:

(i) Derived demand: As stated earlier, when a commodity is demanded for the production of some other commodity instead of its own direct use, its demand is said to be an indirect demand. For instance, the demand for producer's goods and inputs is a derived demand.

(ii) Joint demand: Many times, we use two or more goods together for satisfying a particular want, the demand for such goods is called as joint demand. The demand for complementary goods is a fine example.

(iii) Collective/Composite demand: When a commodity is put to several uses, its total demand in all uses is termed as composite demand. Electricity and water bills are good examples of such a demand.

2.7 Changes in Quantity Demanded Versus Changes in Demand

In economic analysis, 'changes in quantity demanded' and 'changes in demand' **altogether have different meanings**. The changes in quantity demanded relates to the **law of demand** and it has reference to '**extension** ' or '**contraction**' of demand, but the changes in demand is related to '**increase' or 'decrease'** in demand.

Changes in quantity demanded take place only in response to **the own price** of the commodity, while changes in demand take place due to **changes in non-price factors** such as income, taste & preference, price of related goods etc. '**price demand' is an example of changes in quantity demanded and income demand and cross demand represent the case of changes in demand. Price is the driving force** in bringing changes in amount demanded, while **non-price factors** are responsible for the changes in demand.

In graphical depiction, changes in quantity demanded are **shown by the movement along the same demand curve**. A downward movement from one point to another on the same demand curve implies extension of demand, i.e., more quantity is demanded at lower price. Contrary to it, upward movement from one point to another on the same demand curve implies contraction of demand, i.e., less quantity is demanded at higher price.

Changes in demand (increase or decrease), is graphically **depicted by shifting of the demand curve**. In case of an increase in demand, the **demand curve is shifted to the right** and in case of decrease in demand, **the demand curve is shifted to the left**.

Increase in demand: Technically, it may be in the following two forms:
- Higher quantity at the same price,
- Same quantity at higher price

Similarly, **decrease in demand** may also be in following two forms:
- Lesser quantity at the same price.
- Same quantity at lower price.

Changes in quantity demanded (extension and contraction of demand)

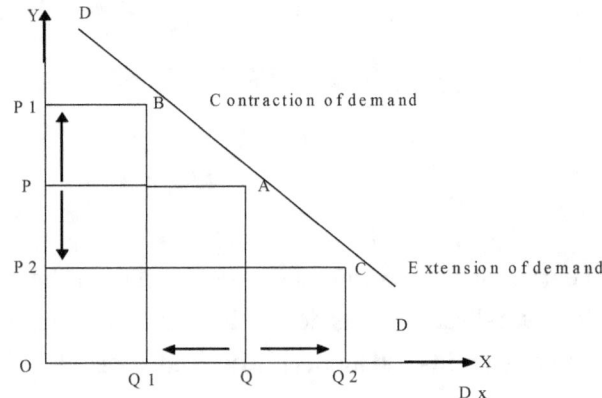

Changes in Demand

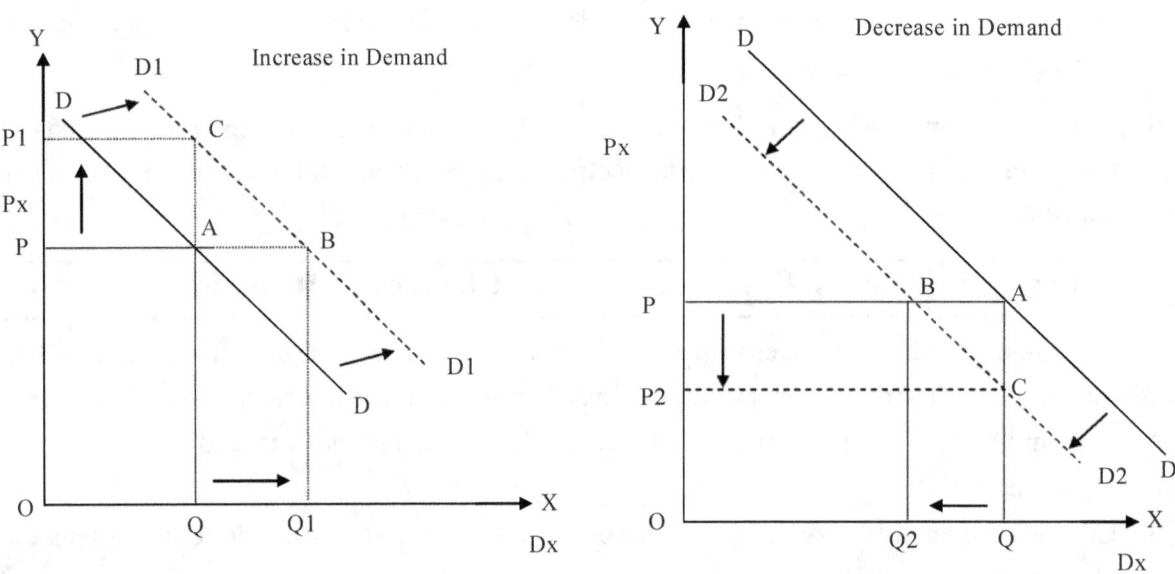

2.8 Summary

Demand is one of the most important economic decision variables. Demand analysis is very crucial for managerial decisions related to market strategy, pricing, advertising, production planning, inventory management, financial evaluation and investment decisions. Demand is effective want related to given price and given time period. The determinants of the demand include both price and non-price factors and they are responsible for bringing changes in quantity demanded and changes in demand. Changes in demand take place only in response to the price of the commodity under consideration in the form of contraction and extension of demand, but the changes in demand is a result of changes in non-price factors which influence the demand for a product. These changes are either as increase in demand or decrease in demand. Price demand, income demand, cross demand, derived demand are some of the important types of demand which are crucial for understanding the law of demand and elasticity of demand. The law of demand states, if other things are equal, there is an inverse relationship between the price of a commodity and its quantity demanded, i.e., higher the price, lower the demand and vice versa. There are only few real exceptiona to the law of demand such as Giffen goods, Veblen goods and articles of bare necessity. In this unit, we are also exposed to various distinct concepts of demand such as new and replacement demand, short-run and long-run demand, perishable and durable goods demand, individual and market demand, domestic and industrial demand etc..

2.9 Key Words

- **Demand:** It is that quantity of a commodity which will be purchased at a given price and at a given time.

- **Price demand:** It expresses those quantities of a commodity, if other things remaining the same, which will be bought by a consumer at its different prices during a specified period of time.

- **Income demand:** It denotes those quantities of a commodity, if other things remaining the same, which will be purchased by a consumer at different levels of his income during a period of time.

- **Cross demand:** It signifies those quantities of a commodity(X), if other things are equal, which will be bought by a consumer at different prices of its related goods(Y).

- **Derived demand:** It is an indirect demand of a commodity which is demanded for producing some other commodity.

- **Joint demand:** It is the demand of those goods which are needed together for satisfying a particular want. For instance, demand for complementary goods.

- **Composite demand:** The total demand of a commodity in its several uses is known as mixed demand. For instance the total demand of electricity for a household.

- **Demand schedule:** It is a statistical/functional relationship of the price of a commodity and its quantity demanded, if other things are equal.

- **Demand function:** It expresses functional relationship between the demand for a commodity and factors influencing the demand. They are also known as demand determinants.

- **Law of demand:** It states an inverse relationship between the price of a commodity and its quantity demanded, if other things are equal, i.e., higher the price, lower the demand and vice-versa.

- **Changes in quantity demanded:** When the quantity purchased of a commodity changes only due to change in its own price, known as changes in quantity demanded. It is either in the form of extension or contraction of demand. Price demand is a good example.

- **Changes in demand:** When quantity bought changes due to changes in other determinants of demand except the price of the commodity under consideration, it is termed as changes in demand. It can be either increase or decrease in demand. Income demand and cross demand are good examples.

- **Price effect:** It is the influence of changes in price of a commodity on its quantity demanded. It is generally negative.

- **Income effect:** It signifies the impact of changes in income of the consumer on the demand for a commodity. It can be positive or negative.

- **Cross effect:** It expresses the impact of changes in price of related goods (Py) on the demand of the parent product.(Dx) It can also be positive or negative.

- **Substitute goods:** Those goods which can easily be used in place of each other for satisfying a particular want. For instance, tea and coffee.

- **Complementary goods:** Those goods which are required together for satisfying a particular want. For instance, tea, sugar& milk or cricket bat and ball.

- **Superior/normal goods:** These are the goods the demand for which increases with increase in income of the consumer and vice-versa.

- **Giffen/inferior goods:** Those goods whose demand declines with increase in income of the consumers. For instance, Coarse grain and clothes.

- **Veblen Effect :** It refers to the desire of a person (usually very rich) to own exclusive or unique product – called veblen good / snob good. It serves as prestige symbol.

- **Bandwagon Effect :** It is also known as demonstration effect : The demand for a product seems to be determined basically not by the utility of it, but mostly on account of consumption of trend setters such as cricket /film stars, models, neighbours etc.

- **Ceteris Paribus** : It means other things being equal. It is a French word

2.10 Self Assessment Test

1. Make a list of factors which may determine the demand for

   (a) a consumer durable item like car / washing machine

   (b) an intermediate good like cables

   (c) a producer good like machinery / equipment

   Analyse the common factors.

2. Draw the following :

   (a) Exceptional Demand Curve

   (b) Income Demand Curve for Superior goods

   (c) Income Demand Curve for Giffin goods

(d) Cross demand curve for Substitute goods

(e) Cross demand curve for complementary goods

3. Distinguish between the following :

(a) Extension of demand and increase in demand

(b) Contraction of demand and decrease in demand

(c) Want and demand

(d) Substitution effect and income effect

(e) Inferior goods and Giffen goods

(f) Direct and derived demand

4. Construct a typical individual and market demand schedule and draw the demand curve based on them

2.11 Suggested Books / References

1. Mithani D.M. : Managerial Economics, Himalaya Publishing House, Mumbai

2. Dwivedi, D.N. : Managerial Economics, Vikas Publishing House Pvt. Ltd, New Delhi

3. Misra & Puri : Economics for Managers, Himalaya Publishing House, Mumbai

4. Adhikary M. : Managerial Economics, Khosla Educational Publishers, Delhi

5. Mote, Paul & Gupta : Managerial Economics – Concepts & Cases, Tata Mc-Graw Hill Publishing Company Ltd., Mumbai

6. Koutsoyiannis, A : Modern Microeconomics, The Macmillan Press Ltd.,, London

3 Elasticity of Demand and Demand Estimates

Unit-structure

3.0   Objectives

After studying this unit you should be able to understand:

- The concept of elasticity of Demand
- Types and degree of elasticity and price elasticity of Demand
- Methods of measuring the elasticity of Demand – Flux's percentage method, Total outlay method, ARC method and point elasticity of demand method.

3.1   Introduction

Demand and supply play an important role in economics as well as in an economy. Therefore this one is a famous saying that if a parrot is taught demand & supply, demand & supply in the answers of the questions it may prove to be a good economist. This proves that demand & supply play a prominent role in the entire economics. With this background, before we discuss the elasticity of demand, it is better that we should know a brief concept of demand. Law of demand only describes direction of change in demand but elasticity of demand describes degree of change in demand.

3.2   Concept of Demand

Generally demand is that commodity which is demanded by the consumer at a certain price and at a time. In a practical life a person uses so many words instead of demand for example- desire, effective desire, wants, needs etc. but in a practical market, the concept is different. We can explain with the help of following chart-

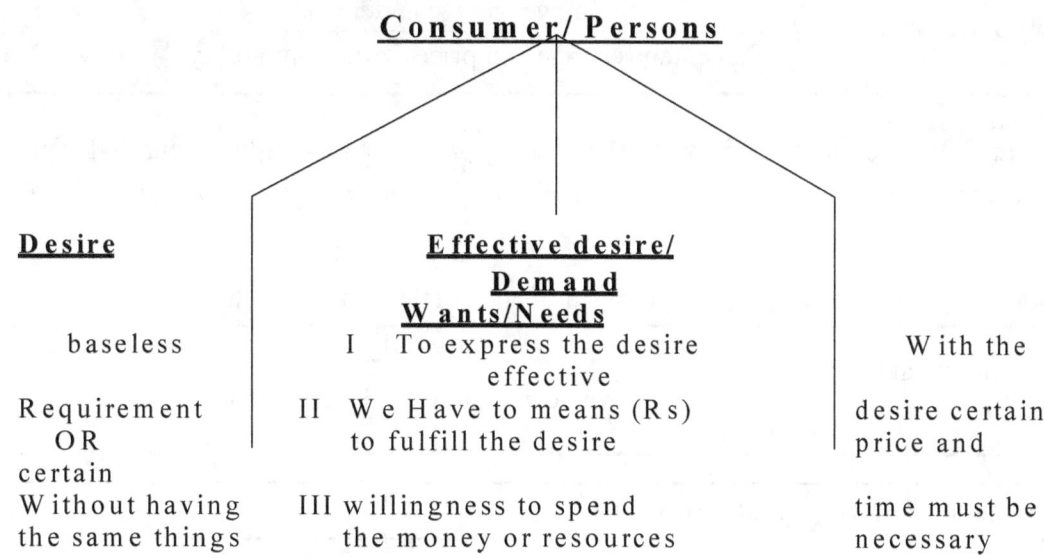

Consumer/ Persons

Desire	Effective desire/ Demand Wants/Needs	
baseless	I To express the desire effective	With the
Requirement OR certain	II We Have to means (Rs) to fulfill the desire	desire certain price and
Without having the same things	III willingness to spend the money or resources	time must be necessary

It is clear from the above discussion that demand is an effective desire at a certain price and at a certain time by consumers in a market.

3.3 Concept of Elasticity of Demand

Background- Law of demand describes the qualitative aspect regarding the inverse relationship between price and demand and elasticity of demand describes the quantitative aspects regarding the inverse relationship between price & demand. We can explain qualitative and quantitative aspects of price & demand with the help of the following chart

CHART

Law of Demand	Elasticity of Demand
Qualitative aspect means we talk about Only inverse relationship between price and demand	Quantitative aspect means we talk about how much percentage change in price and how much percentage change in demand.

Concept of Elasticity of Demand

Other things remaining the same, due to certain percentage change in a price of the commodity if certain percentage changes in demand of that commodity it is known as elasticity of demand. The concept of elasticity of demand is generally associated with the name of Alfred Marshal Though this idea was evolved much earlier by economists like Courrat and Duel different economists have defined the elasticity of demand. Some of the definitions are given below:-

Prof. Alfred Marshal, "The elasticity (or Responsiveness) of demand in a market is large or small according to the amount demanded increases much or little for a given rise in price."

Prof. K.E. Boulding, "The elasticity of demand may be defined as the percentage change in the quantity demand which would result in one percent change in price." Boulding gives the following formula to calculate the elasticity of demand-

$$\text{Elasticity of Demand} = \frac{\text{Percentage change in demand}}{\text{Percentage change in a price of the commodity}}$$

Mrs. John Robinson, "The elasticity of demand at any price or at any output is equal to the proportional change of amount demanded in response to a small change in price divided by the proportional change in price."

Robinson also gives the following formula for calculation of the elasticity of demand.

$$\text{Elasticity of Demand} = \frac{\text{Percentage change in demand}}{\text{Percentage change in a price of the commodity}}$$

3.4 Types of Elasticity of Demand

Before we discuss the types and degree of elasticity of demand it is better if we can express entire structure of types & degree of elasticity of demand with the help of the following chart-

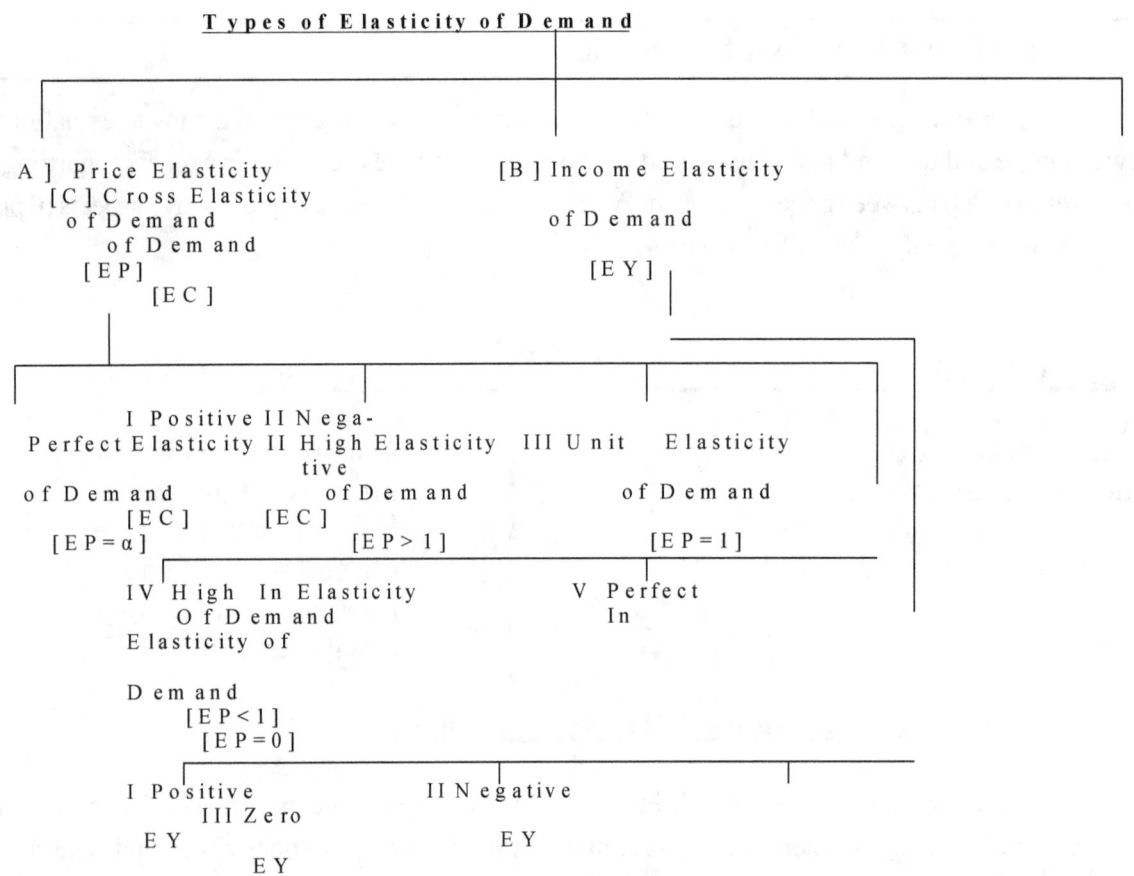

Price Elasticity of Demand (EP)- Other things remaining the same due to certain percentage change in price if certain percentage change in demand of commodity is there, it is known as price elasticity of demand. It is measured as percentage change in quantity demanded divided by the percentage change in price.

$$ED = \frac{\text{Percentage change in Quantity demanded}}{\text{Percentage change in price}}$$

or

Or

$$\frac{\%\Delta\Delta}{\%\Delta\Delta} \quad \frac{\% \quad Q}{\% \quad \triangle P}$$

28

Where Ep = Price Elasticity
    P   = Price
    Q = Quantity
    Δ = Change

3.5 Degree of Price Elasticity of Demand

I Perfectly Elastic Demand (Ep=á):

    When minor, nothing or as good as zero percentage change in price results in tremendous percentage change in demand, it is known as perfectly elastic demand. We can say in other words that it is a situation in which demand of a commodity continuously changes without any change in price. It can be explained with the help of following example and diagram.

Example:-

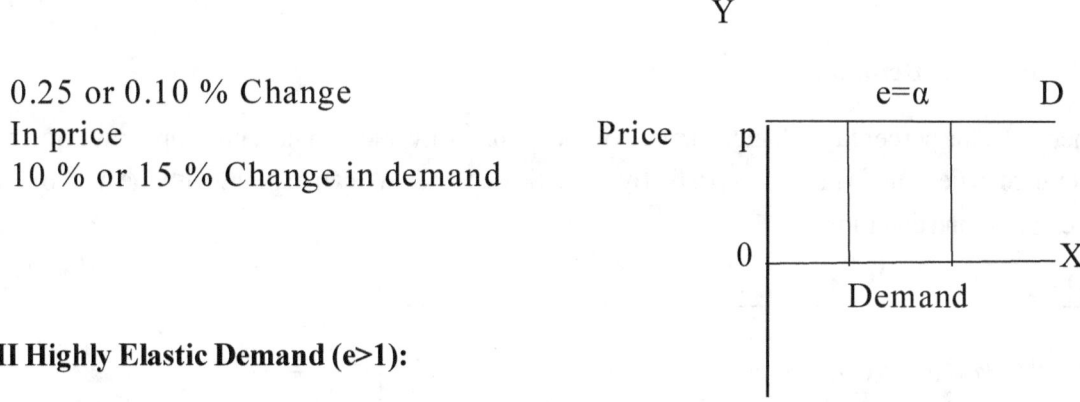

0.25 or 0.10 % Change
In price
10 % or 15 % Change in demand

II Highly Elastic Demand (e>1):

    When less percentage change in price of commodity and if as compared to that more percentage change in demand is there, it is known as highly elastic demand. We can say in other words that it refers to a situation in which percentage change in demand of commodity is higher than percentage change in price of that commodity. We can explain this with the help of the following example and diagram-

Example:-

5% Change In price

20% Change in demand

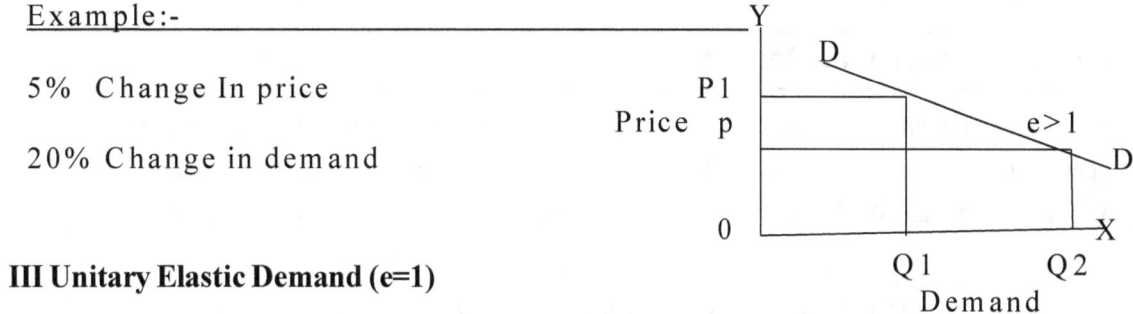

III Unitary Elastic Demand (e=1)

    When equal percentage or a proportionate change in price of commodity and demand of commodity is there, it is known as unitary elastic demand . It means that percentage change in demand of a commodity is equal to percentage change in price. We can explain this with the help of following example and diagram-

Example:-

10% Change In price

10% Change in demand

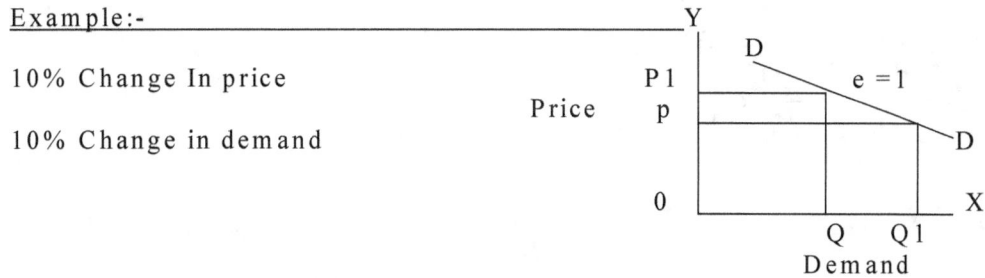

IV Highly Inelastic Demand (e<1)

When as compared to price less percentage change in demand of that particular commodity is there it is known as highly inelastic demand. It means when percentage change in demand of a commodity is less than percentage change in demand in price. We can explain with the help of following example and diagram-

Example:-

20 % Change In price

5 % Change in demand

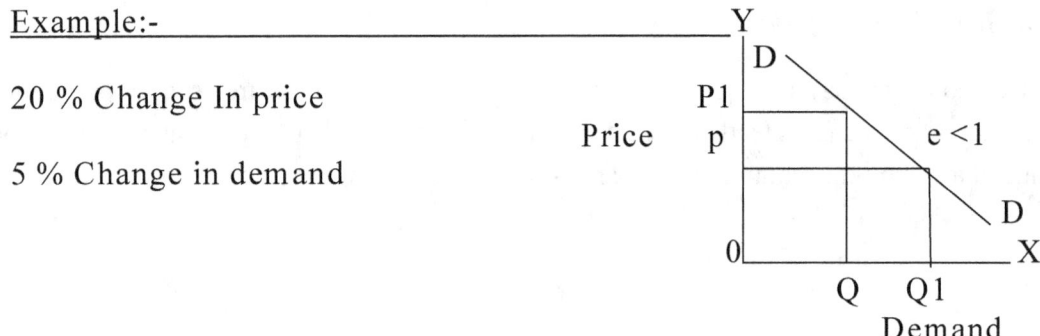

V Perfectly Inelastic Demand (e=0)

When extreme percentage change in price of the commodity and if minor, nothing or as good on zero percentage in demand is known as perfectly inelastic demand. We can explain with the help of the following example and diagram-

Example:-

10% OR 15 %Change In price

0.25 % OR 0.10 % Change in demand

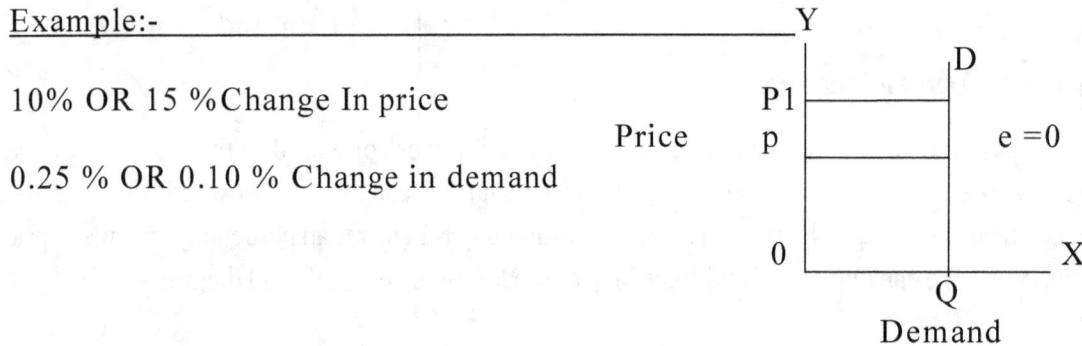

3.6 Income Elasticity of Demand

Other things remaining the same due to certain percentage change in consumer's income if there is certain percentage change in demand it is known as income elasticity of demand. It means the ratio of percentage change in quantity demanded due to percentage change in income of consumers.

$$EY = \frac{Percentage\ change\ in\ Quantity\ demanded}{Percentage\ change\ in\ income}$$

$$\frac{\%\Delta Q}{\%\Delta Y}$$

$$EY = \frac{\Delta Q}{\Delta Y} \times \frac{Y}{Q}$$

Types/ Degree of Income Elasticity

I Positive Income Elasticity –

Increase in normal/ luxury goods, there will be positive relation between income and demand because as income increases demand increase and vice versa. Positive income elasticity may be of three types- EY=1, Ey>1, Ey<1

II Negative Income Elasticity (EY<0)-

Incase of inferior goods, the income elasticity of demand is negative because there will be an inverse relation between income and demand for inferior goods. As income increases demand for inferior goods decreases and vice versa.

III Zero Income Elasticity (EY=0)

In case of necessary goods wehther income increases or decreases the quantity demanded remains the same. So Zero income is found here.

3.7 Cross Elasticity of Demand

Other things remaining the same due to certain percentage change in price of one commodity certain percentage change in demand of another commodity is known as cross elasticity of demand.

$$EC = \frac{\text{Percentage change in Quantity demanded x commodity}}{\text{Percentage change in price x commodity}}$$

OR

$$\frac{\%\Delta QX}{\%\Delta PY}$$

$$EC = \frac{\Delta QX}{\Delta PY} \times \frac{PY}{QX}$$

Types/ Degree of Cross Elasticity

I Positive Cross Elasticity- In case of substitute goods for example – tea and coffee, there is positive relation so Positive Lie between to "

II Negative Cross Elasticity - Incase of complementary goods like car and petrol, there is inverse relation. So negative cross elasticity is found here Negative lie between -0 to - "

3.8 Measuring the Price Elasticity of Demand

[A] Flux's Percentage Method:- Prof. Flux tries to measure the price elasticity of demand with the help of percentage. According to him e=" and e=0 does not exist in practical life and says that e>1, e=1 & e<1 have a practical approach.

According to Prof. Flux "due to certain percentage change in price of commodity if certain percentage change in demand of that particular commodity is there, it is known as price elasticity of demand." Prof. Flux gives the following formula for the calculation of the price elasticity of demand:-

$$EP = \frac{\% \text{ change in Quantity demanded}}{\% \text{ change in price}}$$

Example

$$\frac{20\% \text{ change in Quantity demand}}{10\% \text{ change in price}}$$

$$= \frac{20}{10} = \frac{2}{1}$$

$= e > 1 \text{ elasticity of demand}$

$$\frac{10\% \text{ change in Quantity demand}}{10\% \text{ change in price}}$$

$$= \frac{10}{10} = \frac{1}{1}$$

$= e = 1 \text{ elasticity of demand}$

$$\frac{10\% \text{ change in Quantity demand}}{20\% \text{ change in price}}$$

$$= \frac{10}{20} = \frac{1}{1}$$

$= e < 1 \text{ elasticity of demand}$

[B] Total Outlay/Total Expenditure Method

Prof. Alfred Marshal tries to measure the price elasticity of demand with the help of total expenditure method and he also says that e= and e=0 does not exist in practical life and e>1,e=1 & e<1 have practical approach. Under this method elasticity will be of three types:-

I E> 1 elasticity of demand:- When there is inverse relation between price and total expenditure it means that when price increases total expenditure increases and vice versa , it is known as e>1 elasticity of demand.

II E=1 elasticity of demand:- Even if price increases or decreases but total expenditure is constant, then it is known as e=1 or a unit elasticity of demand.

III E<1 elasticity of demand:- When there is positive or direct relationship between price total expenditure it means as the price increase total expenditure increase & vice versa is known as E<1 elasticity of demand.

We can explain total expenditure method with the help of the following chart and diagram.

CHART
Price change and its effect on Total expenditure

Types	Price Change (p)	Total Expenditure (T E)	Relation
(a) E = 1	↑ OR ↓	No Change	No Relation
(b) E < 1 Inelastic Demand	↑ ↓	↑ ↓	Positive Relation Between P and T E
(c) E > 1 Elastic Demand	↑ ↓	↑ ↓	Negative Relation Between P and T E

32

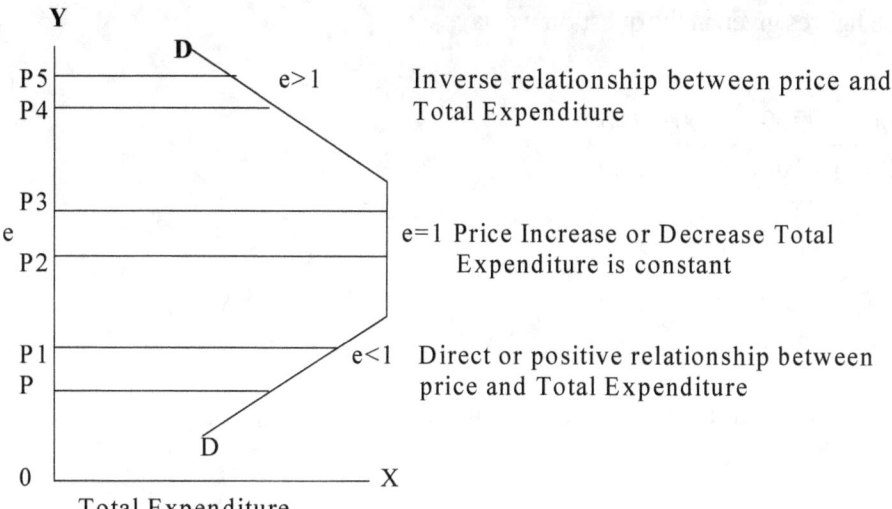

Y

P5 ————————— D   e>1   Inverse relationship between price and
P4 —————————   Total Expenditure

P3 —————————
e   e=1 Price Increase or Decrease Total
P2 —————————   Expenditure is constant

P1 —————————
P —————————   e<1   Direct or positive relationship between
                          price and Total Expenditure

          D
0 ——————————————— X
   Total Expenditure

[C] ARC Elasticity of Demand:-

When we measure any two particular points of the demand curve, it is known as ARC elasticity of demand. When there is a major percentage change in price or in a demand then ARC elasticity of demand method is appropriate for the economist.

In reality we may come across demand schedules which have gaps in prices as well as in quantities. ARC signifies a segment or portion of a curve between two points. The formula for measuring the ARC elasticity is :-

$$Ec = \frac{\dfrac{\text{Original quantity- New quantity}}{\text{Original quantity+New quantity}}}{\dfrac{\text{Original price – New Price}}{\text{Original Price+ New Price}}}$$

$$= \frac{Q\ Q_1}{Q+Q_1} \div \frac{P\ P_1}{P+P_1}$$

$$= \frac{Q\ Q_1}{Q+Q_1} \times \frac{P+P_1}{P\ P_1}$$

$$= \frac{Q\ Q_1}{P+P_1} \div \frac{P+P_1}{Q\ Q_1}$$

In Which –   Q   = Original quantity demanded
         Q_1 = New quantity demanded
         P   = Original Price
         P_1 = New Price

Let us take a concrete example to explain the arc method. The demand when the price was 3000 units per week and the price was Rs. 2/- per unit. The demand contracted to 2700 units when price was raised to Rs. 2.10 per unit. Calculate elasticity of demand by ARC method. The formula is:-

$$Ec = \frac{Q\ Q_1}{Q+Q_1} \div \frac{P\ P_1}{P+P_1}$$

$$= \frac{Q\ Q_1}{Q+Q_1} \times \frac{P+P_1}{P\ P_1}$$

33

Now substituting with the figures given in the question we have

$$Ec = \frac{3000 - 2700}{3000 + 2700} \times \frac{200 + 210}{200 - 210}$$

$$= \frac{300}{5700} \times \frac{410}{10}$$

$$= \frac{41}{19} = 2.16 \, (\text{Minus Symbol May be Omitted})$$

Elasticity of demand is 2.16

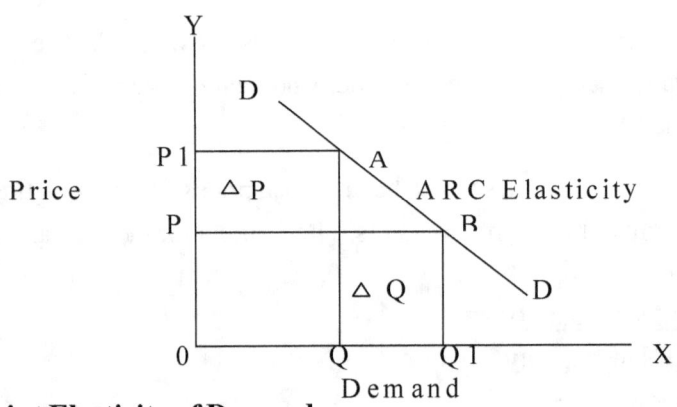

[D] Point Elasticity of Demand:-

When there is minor percentage change in price & demand then point elasticity of demand method is useful for the economist. Price elasticity of demand can also be measured with the help of what is known as the "Point Method." According to this method , elasticity of demand on each point of a demand curve shall be different, and can be measured with the help of the following formula:-

$$\text{Point elasticity of demand} = \frac{\text{Lower Sagment of the demand curve}}{\text{Upper segment of demand curve}}$$

Elasticity at different point of a straight line demand curve by different points use the above formula. We can calculate the elasticity of demand and at any point on a straight line demand curve—

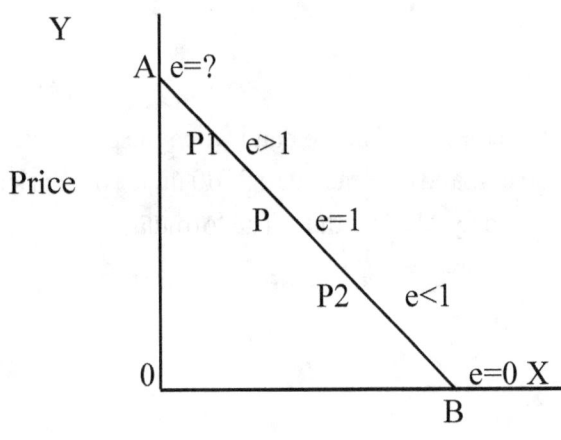

It shall be Zero at the point where the demand curve Touches horizontal axis; and it shall be infinity where it Touched vertical axis. It shall be equal to unity at the central Point of the demand curve.

34

It shall be less than unity in the lower segment and more than unity in the upper segment of the curve. It is equal to unity at the middle point of the curve AB less than unity in the lower segment and more than unity in the upper segment.

It is clear from the above diagram that AB is the straight line demand curve. Let us take price P as the middle point of the demand curve AB.

Now, E at point

$$P = \frac{PB}{PA} = 1 \quad \text{To illustrate the same point}$$

(For PB= PA)

Let us assume AB to represent 6 cm. then the middle point of AB, PB will be equal to 3cm and PA will be equal to 3 cm.

$$\text{E at point } P = \frac{PB}{PA} = \frac{3\,cm}{3\,cm} = 1$$

Let us take a price p1 at the point higher than the middle point of the demand curve AB.

$$\text{E at point } P_1 = \frac{P_1B}{P_1A} = \quad \text{More than 1 (P1B>P1A)}$$

Using the numerical example of AB being equal to 6cm; then

$$\text{E at point } P_1 = \frac{P_1B}{P_1A} = \frac{4\,cm}{2\,cm} = 2 \text{ more than 1}$$

At a price lower than the middle point of the demand curve (P2) elasticity will be less unity as far instance.

$$\text{E at point } P_2 = \frac{P_2B}{P_1B} = \quad \text{Less than 1 (P2B<P2A)}$$

If P2 B is 2 c, and P2A is 4cm ; than

$$\text{E at point } P_2 = \frac{P_2B}{P_2A} = \frac{2\,cm}{4\,cm} \quad 0.5 \text{ Less than 1.}$$

3.9 Factors Influencing Elasticity of Demand

Demand is a function of price, income, taste, hobby, nature of consumer population, govt. policy etc. Elasticity of demand tends to be different for different types of goods it will differ from market to market with this background we can explain the factors influencing elasticity of demand.

1. **Nature of commodity -** These who have no substitute goods will have an inelasticity of demand. The consumers will buy almost a fixed demand whether the price is higher or lower. Demand for luxuries, on the other hand, is elastic in nature.

2. **Different uses of the commodity-** A commodity that has several kinds of uses is apt to be elastic in demand. For each single use demand may be inelastic so that when price of the commodity goes down only a little more is purchased for every use.

3. **Availability of substitute goods-** When there exists a class substitute in the relevant price range, its demand will tend to be elastic. But in respect of commodities having no substitutes, their demand will be the same inelastic.

4. **Consumer's income -** Generally larger the income, the overall demand for commodities tends to be relatively inelastic. The redistribution of income in favour of low income people may tend to make demand for some goods relatively inelastic.

5. **Proportion of expenditure-** Items that constitute a smaller amount of expenditure in a consumer's family budget tend to have a relatively inelastic demand, e.g., a cinegoer who sees a film every fort night is not likely to give it up when the ticket rates are raised. But one who sees a film every alternate day perhaps may cut down his number of films. So is the case with matches, sugar etc.

6. **Durability of the commodity-** In the case of durable goods, the demand generally tends to be inelastic in the short run, e.g., furniture. bicycle radio, etc. In the perishable commodities, on the other hand, demand is relatively elastic, e.g., milk , vegetables, etc.

7. **Influence of habit and customs-** There are certain articles which have a demand on account of conventions, customs or habit and in these cases, elasticity is less, e.g., Mangal Sutra to a Hindu bride or cigarettes to a smoker have inelasticity of demand.

8. **Complementary goods-** Goods which are jointly demanded have less elasticity, e.g., ink, petrol have inelastic demand for this reason.

9. **Recurrence of demand-** If the demand for a commodity is of a recurring nature, its price elasticity is higher than that of a commodity which is purchased only once. For instance, bicycle, tape recorders, radios, etc. are purchased only once, hence their price elasticity will be less. But the demand for cassettes or tape spools would be more price elastic.

10. **Possibility of postponement-** When the demand for a product is postponable, it will tend to be price elastic. In the case of consumption goods which are urgently and immediately required, their demand will be inelastic.

3.10 Importance of Elasticity of Demand

The concept of elasticity of demand is of considerable significance in various situations, which we shall briefly summaries below:

1. **Helpful to a monopolist in fixing price-** The individual producer under imperfect competition has to consider the demand for his product when he fixes its price. He has to take into account the response of his customers in formulating his price policy. Like wise the monopolist has to study the elasticity of demand of his product before he fixes its price.

2. **Helpful to the Government in formulating Taxation Policies-** The concept of elasticity of demand also proves helpful to the Government in the formulation of its economic and taxation policies, The finance minister has to consider the nature of the elasticity of demand for a commodity before levying an excise tax on it.

3. **Helpful in Determination of rewards for factors of Production-** The concept of elasticity of demand also influences the determination of the rewards for factors of production in a private enterprise economy. If the demand for labour on a particular industry is relatively inelastic, it will be easier for the trade union to get their wages raised. The same remarks apply to other factors of production whose demands are relatively inelastic.

36

4. **Helpful in determination of terms of trade-** It is possible to calculate the terms of trade between two countries only by taking into account the mutual elasticities of demand for each others products. The term "Terms of Trade" implies the rate at which one unit of a domestic commodity will exchange for units of commodity of a foreign country.

5. **Helpful in determining the Rate of Exchange-** The concept of elasticity of demand also helps the government in fixing an appropriate foreign rate of exchange for its domestic currency in relation to the currencies of other countries. Before deciding to devalue or revalue domestic currency in relation to foreign currencies the government has to study carefully the elasticites of demand for its imports and exports.

6. **Helpful in declaring certain industries as 'Public Utilities'-** The concept of elasticity of demand also enables the government to decide as to what particular industries should be declared as public utilities and being consequently owned and operated by state.

3.11 Summary

Demand & law of demand is related with the Qualitative aspect regarding the inverse relationship between price & demand and elasticity of demand is related with the Quantitative aspect regarding the inverse relationship between price and demand. Elasticity of demand means due to certain percentage change in price if certain percentages change in Quantity demand by consumers.

Price elasticity of demand is a measure of the extent to which quantity demanded of a good responds to a change in its price. When the numerical measure is less then one, we say that the demand is inelastic. When it is e>1, we say demand is elastic and when it is e=1 we say demand is unitary Two special cases are when elasticity equals zero (e=0) or infinity (e="). When elasticity is (e=0), the quantity demanded does not change at all as price changes, and when elasticity e=", a very small reduction in price increases the quantity demanded from zero to an infinity large number.

Price elasticity can be measured at a point or between two points Here we use the concepts of point elasticity and ARC elasticity respectively. The main determinants of elasticity are the availability of substitutes for the commodity, numbers of uses of the commodity, nature of commodity etc.

3.12 Self Assessment Test

1. What do you mean by elasticity of demand? Explain various types of demand elasticity with illustrations.
2. What are the various factors affecting price elasticity of demand?
3. Discuss the various methods of measuring the elasticity of demand.
4. Write a short note on the following points :-
   A. Total Expenditure Method
   B. ARC elasticity of demand Method.
5. Discuss the degree of price elasticity of demand with the help of example and diagram.

3.13 Suggested Books/References

1. Dwivedi, D.N. : Managerial Economics, Himalaya Publishing House, Mumbai.

2. Mate, Paul & Gupta : Managerial Economics-concept & cases tala Mc Grow Hill publication company limited, Mumbai

4 Demand Forecasting

Unit Structure

4.0 Objectives

Under dynamic business conditions demand forecasting is very difficult. It is also difficult in case of new products about which no information is available about consumer's preferences. In this chapter. we shall discuss the purpose of demand forecasting, scope, steps and methods of demand forecasting.

4.1 Introduction

Generally, there is uncertainity in over every decision-making process. The producer of some goods or any other decision-making authority or the government must keep in view the existing level of demand for the product in question and estimate the prevalent gap between demand and supply. The decision maker, whether a firm or a state planning agency, must not only estimate the present level of demand but also forecast the demand for a future date.

Degree of risk depends upon the nature of business. All the risks can not be completely eradicated but by proper planning these risks can be minimized. Demand forecasting is also one of the techniques to minimize the risk and uncertainity.

4.2 Concept of Demand Forecasting

Forecasting of demand is the art of predicting demand for a product or a service at some future date on the basis of certain present and past behaviour patterns of some related events. Please remember that forecasting is no simple guessing but it refers to estimating scientifically and objectively on the basis of certain facts and events relevant to the art of forecasting.

Cundif and Still:-   " According to Cundif and Still sales forecasting is an estimate of sales during a specified future period on which estimates is tied to a proposed marketing plan which assumes a particular set of uncontrollable and competitive forces."

According to Philip Kotler:- " The Company sales forecast is the expected level of company sales based on a chosen marketing plan and assumed marketing environment."

4.3 Features of Demand Forecasting

From the above discussions the following features of demand forecasting emerge:

1. Demand forecasting is based on past data and present positions.

2. Demand forecasting may be monetary or physical.

3. Demand forecasting gives basis to future planning.

4. Demand forecasting is made for a certain period.

5. Future sales and profit estimate can be made by demand forecasting.

4.4 Importance of Demand Forecasting

Demand forecasting is important for every producer. He has to know the present level of demand as also the increase that is expected to take place in the demand for his product over time. Demand forecasts are generally useful for the following categories of decision makers:-

1. Importance for the producers.
2. Importance for policy makers and planners.
3. Importance for estimating financial requirements.
4. Utility for determination of sales target & incentive.
5. Importance for regular supply of labour and raw material is made possible by demand forecasting.
6. Production planning is possible with the help of demand forecasting.
7. Use for other groups of the society researchers, social workers and other who have a futuristic approach.

4.5 Scope of Demand Forecasting

Demand forecasting can be at the international level depending upon the area of operation of given economic institution. It can also be confined to a given product or service supplied by a small firm in local area. The scope of work will depend upon the area of operation in the present and proposed in future much would depend upon the cost and time involved in relation to the benefit of the information acquired through the study of demand. The factors determining the scope of demand forecasting are as follows:-

1. Period conversed under demand forecasting.
2. Levels of demand forecasting.
3. Purpose of demand forecasting.
4. Nature of product.
5. Miscellaneous factors- socio-psychological factors, degree of competition impact of risk and uncertainity.

4.6 Methods of Demand Forecasting

Demand forecasting is a very absorbing and difficult exercise. Consumer's behaviour is the most unpredictable thing in the world because it is motivated and influenced by multiplicity. Moreover; economist and statisticians over the years have developed several methods of demand forecasting. Each of these methods has its relative merits and demerits. Selection of the right method is essential to make demand forecasting accurate and credible. The methods of demand forecasting can be summarized in the form of a chart as follows:-

CHART
Methods of Demand Forecasting

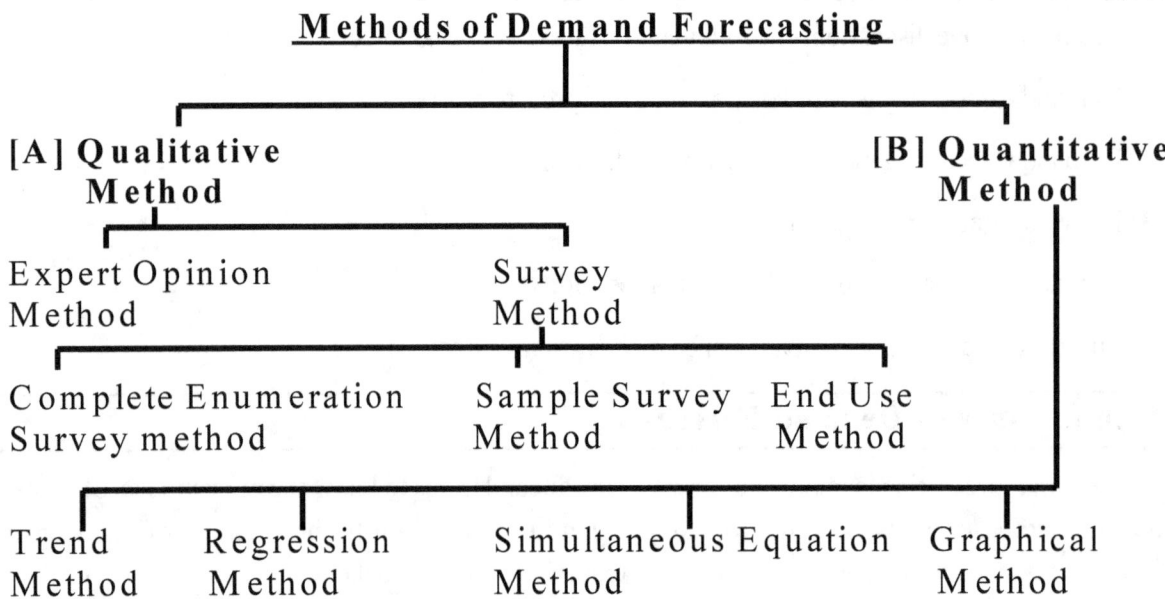

[A] **Qualitative Method**:-

Expert Opinion Method:- Under this method the researcher identifies the experts on the commodity whose demand forecast is being attempted and probes with them on the likely demand for the product in the forecast period. The word 'Expert' is a high powered term but it should be taken to stand for those who possess the requisite expertise on the subject.

A specialised form of panel opinion is the Delphi method, Instead of going in for direct identification. This method seeks the opinion of a group of experts through mail about the expected level of demand. The responses so received are analysed by an independent body. The method thus takes care of the disadvantage of panel consensus where some powerful individual could have influenced the consensus.

Survey Method:- According to this method a few consumers are selected and their views on the probable demand are collected. The sample is considered to be a true representation of the entire population. The demand of the sample so ascertained is then magnified to generate the total demand of all the consumers for that commodity in the forecast period. The selection of an opinion sample size is crucial to this method, while a small sample would be easily managed and less costly.

Enumeration Survy Method:- Under this technique either consumers are divided in several groups on the basis of income, caste, sex, education or any other variable or they may be divided according to geographical regions. Through appropriately selected sample design, sample units are selected and data are collected either through direct interview or by mailing questionnaires or filling up schedules. The results of sample survey may be reliable provided the sample is representative of the population.

Sample Survey Method:- Under this method only a few consumers are selected and their views on the probable demand are collected. The sample is considered to by a true representation of the entire population. The demand of the sample so ascertained is then magnified to generate the total demand of all consumers for that commodity in the forecast period.

End Use Survey Method:- Under this method commodity that is used for the production of some other finally consumable goods is also known as an intermediary good. While the demand for goods used for final consumption can be forecasted using any other method the end use method focuses on forecasting the demand for intermediary goods. Such goods can also be exported or imported besides being used for domestic production of other goods. For example milk is a commodity which can be used as an intermediary good for the production of ICE Cream, paneer and other dairy products. We can analyze end use method with the help of following formula:-

$$Dm = Dmc + Dme - Im + X1 .OI + XP. OP + - - - + XN + ON$$

where -

Dme = Export Demand for Milk

Im = Import of Milk

XI = Per Unit Milk Requirement- of the ICE- Cream Industry

OI = Output of ICE Cream Industry

Xp and Op Notations are similar to XI and OI for paneer

The equation above can be generalized to calculate the projected demand for any commodity.

$$D = Dc + De - I + X1.O1 + X2 — XN + ON$$

[B] Quantitative Methods:-

These method is based on historical Quantitative data. A statistical concept is applied to this existing data about the demand for a commodity over the past year in order to generate the predicted demand in the forecast period. Due to this reason these Quantitative methods are also known as statistical methods. Following are the Quantitative methods:-

Trend Projection Method: A firm which has been in existence for some time will have accumulated considerable data on sales pertaining to different time periods. Such data when arranged chronologically yield time series. Time series relating to sales represent the past pattern of effective demand for a particular product.

Such data can be used to project the trend of the time series. This can be done either through graph or through least square method. Following equation is used under Trend Projection Method:-

I $Y = a + bx$

II $Y = Na + B "X$

III   " $XY = a" X + b "X2$

We can explain with the help of following example-

Years	Sales (In Rs. Lacs)
2004	120
2005	140
2006	150
2007	140
2008	170

Q. Findout the estimated sales for neat five year i.e. 2009 to 2013.

41

Solution

Years (N)	Sales (Y)	Deviation (X)	x2	XY
2004	120	-2	4	-240
2005	140	-1	1	-140
2006	150	0	0	0
2007	140	+1	1	140
2008	170	+2	4	340
N=5	? Y =720	? X=0	? x2= 10	? XY =100

Calculation of a ,we have equation (II)

Y=NA+b"X

720= 5a+0

.. a =720/5 = 144

For finding b, we use equation =(III)

"XY=a"X+b"X2

100= 0+ B10

100/0=b

.

.. b=10

By keeping the value of a & b in equation (I)

Y = a+bx (a=144, b=10)

Y= 144+10X (IV)

On the basis of this equation (IV) we can find trend for next five years as follows:-

Years	Deviation (X)	Sales (In Rs. Lacs)	Y=144+10X
2004	-2	-	
2005	-1	-	
2006	0	-	
2007	+1	-	
2008	+2	-(Already Given)	
2009	+3	Y(144+10(3)=174	
2010	+4	184	
2011	+5	194	
2012	+6	204	
2013	+7	214	

Regression Method:- Under this method relationship is established between Quantity demanded and one or more independent variables such as income, price of the related goods, price of the commodity under consideration, advertisement cost etc. In regression a Quantitative relationship is established between demand which is a dependent variable and the independent variable i.e., determinants of demand.

Let us suppose that we have two variables Y and X where Y is dependent on X. it can be expressed in the form of an equation as follows:-

Y=a+bx

We can explain the regression method with the help of following example-

Year	2005	2006	2007	2008	2009
I Income Index	100	110	140	150	200
II Sales of TV (000)	110	130	150	160	180

We are required to estimate sales of T.V. if the Index of income rises to 240. The regression equations will be calculated as follows:

Year	Income Index(X)	Sales of TY (Y)	X_1	Y_1	$X_1 2$	$X_1 Y_1$
2005	100	110	10	11	100	110
2006	110	130	11	13	121	143
2007	140	150	14	15	196	210
2008	150	160	15	16	225	240
2009	200	180	20	18	400	360
			$?X_1=$ 70	$?Y_1$ 73	$?X_1 2$ 1042	$?X_1 Y_1=$ 1063

In order to estimate the regression line we should first find the values of the constants a and b

$$b = \frac{n\Sigma X_1 Y_1 \quad (\Sigma X_1 \Sigma Y_1)}{n\Sigma X_1^2 \quad (\Sigma X_1)_2}$$

$$= \frac{5 \times 1063 \quad (70 \times 73)}{5 \times 1042 \quad (70)^2} = 0.66$$

$$a = \frac{\Sigma Y_1 \quad b \quad \Sigma X_1}{n}$$

$$\frac{73 \quad 70(.66)}{5} = 5.36$$

Hence the regression equation is

Y=a+bx

Or

Y = 5.36+0.66 x

If the Index of Income rises to 240 sales of TV will be estimated as follows:-

Y= 53.6+0.66x240

= 53.6+158.4

= 212 Thousand.

Simultaneous Equations Method- This method, also called the complete system approach to forecasting, is the most sophisticated econometric method of forecasting. Since it involves complicated mathematical and statistical tools, its detail discussion is beyond the scope of this text. Thus the simultaneous equations method overcomes the major problem of the regression method, viz., forecasts for the independent variable.

Graphical Method- Under this method trend is estimated with the help of a graph. Time & Quantity demanded are taken on both the axis and demand forecasting is made for future. This method is completely subjective, as in this method graph is drawn and on the basis of this graph demand forecasting is made Expansion of this graph is completely imaginary & subjective so it can be different for different persons.

According to graphical method, the past data will be plotted on a graph and the indentified trend/ behaviour will be extended further in the same pattern to ascertain the demand in the forecast period. The following diagram shows the past data in bold lines and the forecasted data in dotted lines.

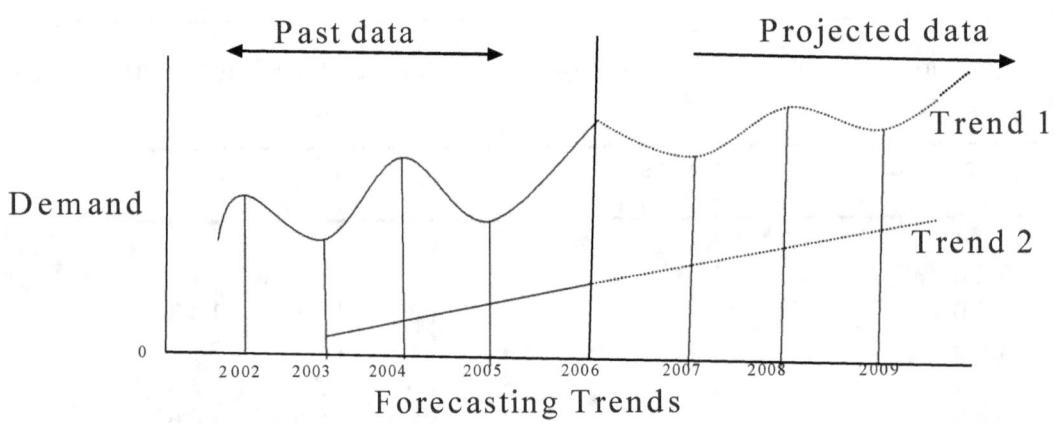

4.7 Demand Forecasting Process

Process for demand forecasting depends on the scope of demand forecasting. We may follow the following sequence in projecting the demand for a product:

1. **Specifying the objectives-** The person or agency assigned the task of forecasting the demand must specifiy the purpose for which demand forecasts are being made.

2. **Selection of Appropriate Method-**Once the purpose of demand forecasting has been specified, we must select the methods which will be used for the purpose.

3. **Collection of Appropriate Data-**The quality and adequacy of data will determine the quality of our results and their reliability. As far as possible, data must be collected by experienced persons.

4. **Estimation and Interpretation of results-** Having collected the relevant data we have to compile them and obtain results manually or with the help of computers. These results must be interpreted and their correspondence with the objective examined.

5. **Evaluation of the Forecasts-** If the method or model used in demand forecasting has objectivity; we may expect to receive good results. Yet the result so obtained must be verified by persons having professional acumen and expertise.

4.8 Summary

Demand forecasting is the art of predicting demand for a product or service at some future date on the basis of certain present and past behavior pattern of some related events. The scope of demand forecasting is determined by nature of the product, time period covered and levels of forecasting

The various methods of demand forecasting are opinion survey, trend analysis, regression analysis etc. The choice depends upon number of factors like nature of the product, cost and time requirements nature of the study etc.

4.9 Self Assessment Test

1.   What is demand forecasting? Explain its scope and importance.

2.   What are the various methods of demand forecasting?

3.   Why is forecasting important to business decisions? Discuss the Qualitative and Quantitative methods of demand forecasting.

4.   Explain the various types of methods of demand forecasting.

5.   Write short notes on:
      (A) Trend Method
      (B) Regression Method
      (C) Graphic Method

4.10 Suggested Books /References

1.   Mathur N.D., Managerial Economics, Shivam book House (P.) Limited, Jaipur
2.   Mithani, D.M. : Managerial Economics, Himalaya Publishing House, Mumbai

5 Production Function

Unit Structure

5.0 Objectives

After studying this unit, you should be able to understand:

- The concept of production function
- The objective, assumption and nature of production function
- Short run production function
- Long run production Function
- The law of variable proportions
- Returns to scale

5.1 Introduction

Production in economic terms is generally understood as the transformation of inputs into outputs. The inputs are what the firm buys, namely productive resources, and outputs are what it sells. Production is not the creation of matter but it is the creation of value. Production is also defined as producing goods which satisfy some human want. Production is a sequence of technical processes requiring either directly or indirectly the mental and physical skill of craftsman and consists of changing requiring either directly or indirectly the mental and physical skill of craftsman and consists of changing the shape, size and properties of materials and ultimately converting them into more useful articles. Means of production refer to the concept which combines the means of labor and the subject of labor. Means of labor simply means all the things which require labor to transform it. Subject of labor means the material to work on. Production, therefore, is the combined resources and equipment needed to come up with goods or services.

Fixed and variable input: An input is the production of goods and services that does not change in the short run. A fixed input should be compared with a variable input, an input that changes in the short run. Fixed and variable inputs are most important for the analysis of short-run production by a firm. The best example of a fixed input is the factory, building, equipment, or other capital used in production. The comparable example of a variable input would then be the labor or workers who work in the factory or operate the equipment. In the short run (such as a day or so) a firm can vary the quantity of labor, but the quantity of capital is fixed.

Short run: A production period of time in which at all inputs in the production process are fixed, meaning the quantity of output itself is fixed. Also termed market period, the short run exists if the period is so short that no additional production is possible. In other words, the good have been produced all that remains is to sell them.

Long run: A production time period in which all inputs are variable, including those under control of the firm and those beyond the control of the firm. During the very long run, not only are the labor, capital, land, and entrepreneurship inputs variable, but so too are key production inputs such as government rules, technology, and social customs.

In other words we can say that production in economics is all those activities that have to do with the creation of commodities, by imparting to raw materials utility, added value, or the ability to satisfy human wants.

5.2 Objective of Production Function

The objective of production function is as under:-

- The primary purpose of the production function is to address allocative efficiency in the use of factor inputs in production and the resulting distribution of income to those factors.

- Production function is a function that specifies the output of a firm for all combinations of inputs.

- The relationship of output to inputs is non-monetary; that is, a production function relates physical inputs to physical outputs, and prices and costs are reflected in the function.

- Influences economic decision-making.

5.3 The Production Function

The production function expresses a functional relationship between quantities of inputs and outputs. It shows how and to what extent output changes with variations in inputs during a specified period of time. In the words of Stigler, "The production function is the name given to the relationship between rates of input of productive services and the rate of output of product. It is the economist's summary of technical knowledge." Basically, the production function is a technological or engineering concept which can be expressed in the form of a table, graph and equation showing the amount of output obtained from various combinations of inputs used in production, given the state of technology. Algebraically, it may be expressed in the form of an equation as

$$Q = f(L, M, N, K, T)$$

Where Q stands for the output of a good per unit of time, L for labour, M for management (or organization), N for land (or natural resources), K for capital and T for given technology, and f refers to the functional relationship.

The production function with many inputs cannot be depicted on a diagram. Moreover, given the specific values of the various inputs, it becomes difficult to solve such a production function mathematically. Economists, therefore, use a two input production function. If we take two inputs, labour and capital, the production function assumes the form

$$Q = f(L, K)$$

The production function as determined by technical conditions of production is of two types: it may be rigid or flexible. The former relates to the short run and the latter to the long run.

The Nature of Production Function

The production function depends upon the following factors:
a) The quantities of inputs to be used.
b) The state of technical knowledge.
c) The possible processes of production.
d) The size of the firm.
e) The prices of inputs.

Now if these factors change the production function automatically changes.

Attributes of Production Function

The following are the important attributes of production function:
i. The production function is a flow concept.
ii. A production function is a technical relationship between inputs and outputs expressed in physical terms.
iii. The production function of a firm depends on the state of technology and inputs.
iv. From the economic point of view, a rational firm is interested not in all the numerous possible levels of output but only in that combination which yields maximum outputs.
v. The short run production function pertains to the given scale of production. The long run production function pertains to the changing scale of production.

5.4 Production Function as Graph

Any of these equations can be plotted on a graph. A typical (quadratic) production function is shown in the following diagram under the assumption of a single variable input (or fixed ratios of inputs so the can be treated as a single variable). All points above the production function are unobtainable with current technology, all points below are technically feasible, and all points on the function show the maximum quantity of output obtainable at the specified level of usage of the input. From the origin, through points A, B, and C, the production function is rising, indicating that as additional units of inputs are used, the quantity of outputs also increases. Beyond point C, the employment of additional units of inputs produces no additional outputs (in fact, total output starts to decline); the variable input is being used too intensively. With too much variable input use relative to the available fixed inputs, the company is experiencing negative returns to variable inputs, and diminishing total returns. In the diagram this is illustrated by the negative marginal physical product curve (MPP) beyond point Z, and the declining production function beyond point C.

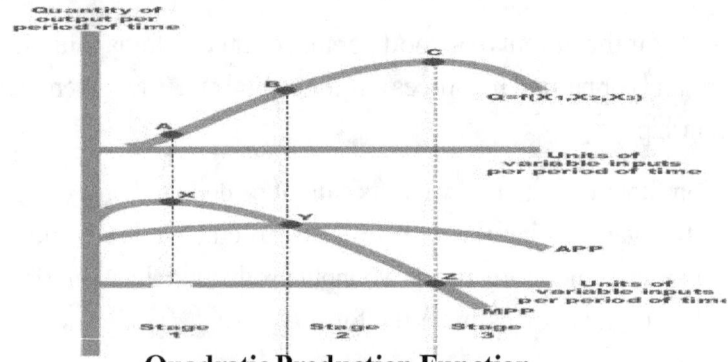

Quadratic Production Function

48

From the origin to point A, the firm is experiencing increasing returns to variable inputs. As additional inputs are employed, output increases at an increasing rate. Both marginal physical product (MPP, the derivative of the production function) and average physical product (APP, the ratio of output to the variable input) are rising. The inflection point A defines the point beyond which there are diminishing marginal returns, as can be seen from the declining MPP curve beyond point X. From point A to point C, the firm is experiencing positive but decreasing marginal returns to the variable input. As additional units of the input are employed, output increases but at a decreasing rate. Point B is the point beyond which there are diminishing average returns, as shown by the declining slope of the average physical product curve (APP) beyond point Y. Point B is just tangent to the steepest ray from the origin hence the average physical product is at a maximum. Beyond point B, mathematical necessity requires that the marginal curve must be below the average curve

5.5 Short Run Production Function

In the short run, the technical conditions of production are rigid so that the various inputs used to produce a given outputs are in fixed proportions. However, in the short run, it is possible to increase the quantities of one input while keeping the quantities of other inputs constant in order to have more output. This aspect of the production function is known as the Law of Variable Proportions. The short run production function in the case of two inputs, labour and capital with capital as fixed and labour as the variable input can be expressed as

$$Q = f(L,R)$$

Where $\bar{K}$ refers to the fixed input.

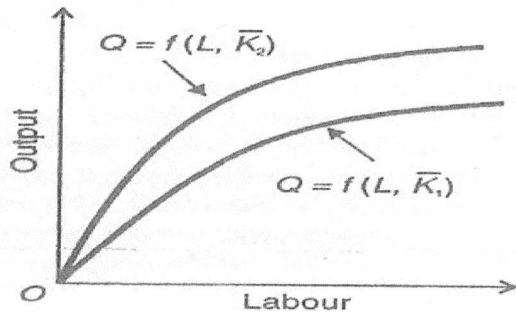

This production function is depicted in Figure 1 where the slope of the curve shows the marginal production of labor. A movements along the production function shows the increase in outputs as labour increases, given the amount of capital employed $\ddot{K}_1$, If the amount of capital increases to $\ddot{K}_2$, at a point of time, the production function $Q = f(L,\bar{K}_1)$ shifts upwards to $Q = f(L,\bar{K}_2)$, as shown in the figure.

On the other hand, if labour is taken as a fixed input and capital as the variable input, the production function takes the form

$$Q = f(KL)$$

This production function is depicted in Figure 2 where the slope of the curve represents the marginal product of capital.

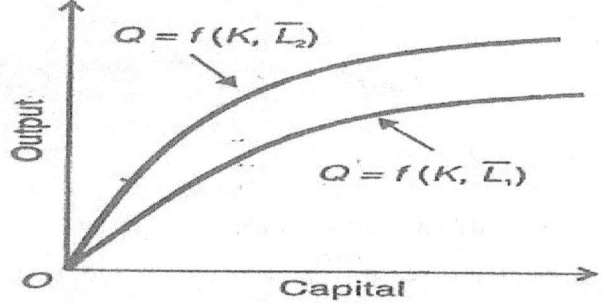

A movement along the production function shows the increase in output as capital increases, given the quantity of labour employed, L_1. If the quantity of labour increases to L_2, at a point of time, the production function $Q = f(K, \ddot{L}_1)$ shifts upwards to $Q = f(K, \ddot{L}_2)$

5.6 Long Run Production Function

In the long run all inputs are variable. Production can be increased by changing one or more of the inputs. The firm can changes its plants or scale of production. Equations (1) and (2) represent the long-run production function. Given the level of technology, a combination of the quantities of labour and capital produces a specified level of output. The long run production function is depicted in Figure 3 where the combination of OK of capital and OL of labour produced 100Q. With the increase in inputs of capital and labour to and , the output increases to 200Q. The long run production function is shown in terms of an isoquant such as 100 Q.

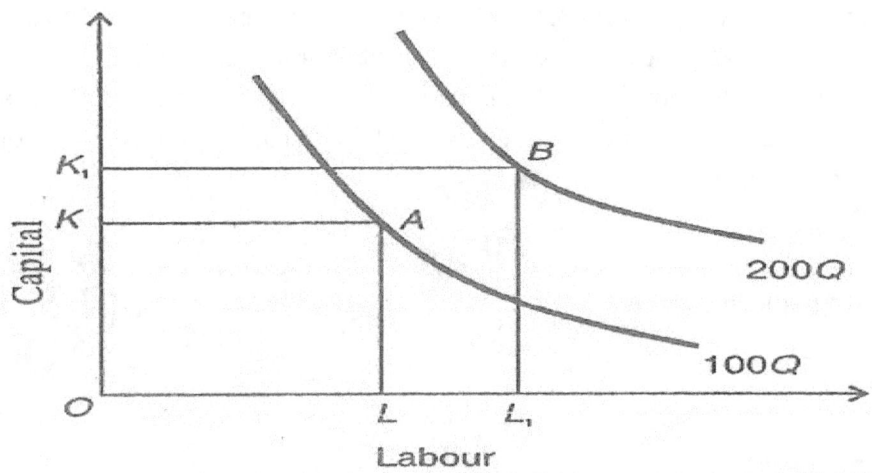

In the long run, it is possible for a firm to change all to change all inputs up or down in accordance with its scale. This is known as returns to scale. The returns to scale are constant when output increases in the same proportion as the increase in the quantities of inputs. The returns to scale are increasing when the increased in output is more than proportional to the increase in inputs. They are decreasing if the increase in output is less than proportional to the increase in inputs.

Let us illustrate the case of constant returns to scale with the help of our production function.

$$Q = (L,\ M,\ N,\ K\ T_2)$$

Given , if the quantities of all inputs L,M,N,K are increased n-fold the output Q also increases n-fold. Then the production function becomes

$$nQ = f(nL,\ nM,\ nN,\ nK\ )$$

This is known as linear an homogeneous production function, or a homogeneous function of the first degree. If the homogeneous function is of the kth degree, the production function is

$$n^k\ Q = f(nL,\ nM,\ nN,\ nK)$$

If k is equal to 1, it is a case of constant returns to scale; if it is greater than 1, it is a case of increasing returns of scale; and if it is less than 1, it is a case of decreasing returns to scale.

Thus a production function is of two types: (i) Liear homogeneous of the first degree in which the output would change in exactly the same proportion as the change in inputs. Doubling the inputs would exactly double the output, and vice versa. Such a production function expresses constant returns to scale. (ii) Non homogeneous production functions of a degree greater or less than one. The former relates to increasing returns to scale and the latter to decreasing returns to scale.

5.7 The Law of Variable Proportions

I   If one input is variable and all other inputs are fixed the firm's production function exhibits the law of variable proportions. If the number of units of a variable factor is increased, keeping other factors constant, how output changes is the concern of this law. Suppose land, plant and equipment are the fixed factors, and labour the variable factor. When the number of laborers in increase successively to have larger output, the proportion between fixed and variable factors is altered and the law of variable proportions sets in. The law states that as the quantity of a variable input is increased by equal doses keeping the quantities of other inputs constant, total product will increase, but after a point at a diminishing rate. This principle can also be defined thus: When more and more units of the variable factor are used, holding the quantities of fixed factors constant, a point is reached beyond which the marginal product, then the average and finally the total product will diminish. The law of variable proportions (or the law of non proportional returns) is also known as the law of diminishing returns. But as we shall see below, the law of diminishing returns is only one phase of the more comprehensive law of variable proportions.

Its Assumptions

The law of diminishing returns is based on the following assumptions:

1) Only one factor is variable while others are held constant.

2) All units of the variable factor are homogeneous.

3) There is no change in technology.

4) It is possible to vary the proportions in which different inputs are combined.

5) It assumes a short run situation, for in the long run all factors are variable.

The product is measured in physical units, i.e. in quintals, tones etc. The use of money in measuring the product may show increasing rather than decreasing returns if the prices of the product rise, even though the output might have declined

Its Explanation

Given these assumptions, let us illustrate the law with the help of Table 1, where on the fixed input land of 5 acres, units of the variable input labour are employed and the resultant output is obtained. The production function is revealed in the first two columns. The average product and marginal product columns are derived from the total product column. The average product per worker is obtained by dividing column (2) by a corresponding unit in column (1). The marginal product is the addition to total product by employing an extra worker. 3 workers produce 36 units and 4 produce 48 units. Thus the marginal product is 12 i.e. (48-36) units.

51

Table. : Output of Wheat in Physical Units (Quintals)

	(1) No. of Workers	(2) Total Product	(3) Average Product	(4) Marginal Product
	1	8	8	8
	2	20	10	12
Stage I				
	3	36	12	16
	4	48	12	12
	5	55	11	7
Stage II				
	6	60	10	5
	7	60	8.6	0
Stage III				
	8	56	7	-4

Products increase at first, reach a maximum and then start declining. The total product reaches its maximum when 7 units of labour are used and then it declines. The average product continues to rise till the 4 the unit while the marginal product reaches its maximum at the 3rd unit of labour, then they also fall. It should be noted that the point of falling output is not the same for total, average and marginal product. The marginal product starts declining first, the average product following it and the total product is the last to fall. This observation points out that the tendency to diminishing returns is ultimately found in the three productivity concepts.

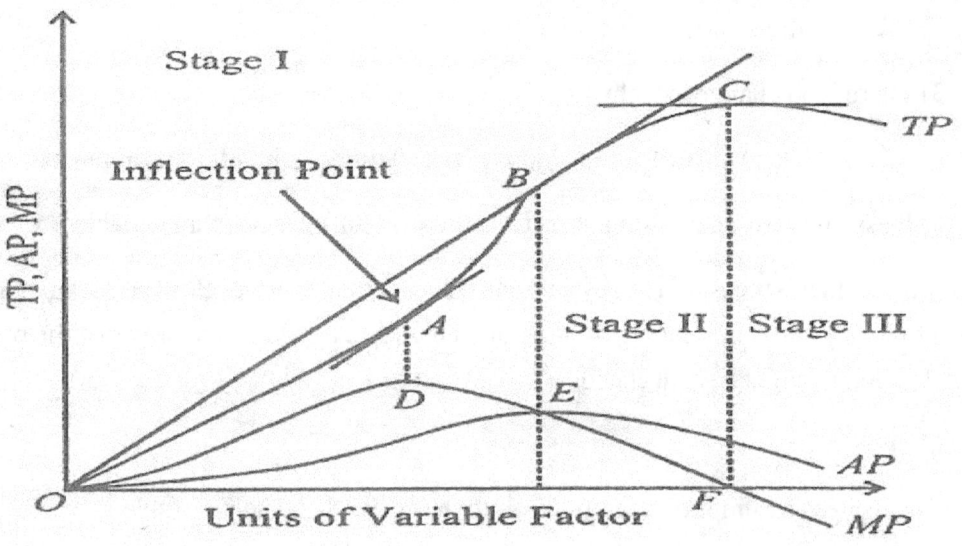

The law of variable proportions is presented diagrammatically in Figure 4. The TP curve first rises at an increasing rate up to point A where its slope is the highest. From point A upwards, the total product increases at a diminishing rate till it reaches its highest point C and then it starts falling. Point A where the tangent touches the TP curve is called is called the inflection point up to which the total product increases at an increasing rate and from where it starts increasing at a diminishing rate. The marginal product curve

(MP) and the average product curve (AP) also rise with TP. the MP curve reaches its maximum point D when the slope of the TP curve is the maximum at point A. The maximum point on the AP curves is E where it coincides with the MP curve. This point also coincides with point B on TP curve from where the total product starts a gradual rise. When the TP curve reaches its maximum point C the MP curve becomes zero at point F. When TP starts declining, The MP curve becomes negative. It is only when the total product is zero that the average product also becomes zero. The rising, the falling and the negative phases of the total, marginal and average products are in fact the different stages of the law of variable proportions which are discussed below.

Three Stages of Production

Stage - I : Increasing Returns: In stage I the average product reaches the maximum and equals the marginal product when 4 workers are employed, as shown in the table 1. This stage is portrayed in the figure from the origin to point E where the MP curve reaches its maximum and the AP curve is still rising. In this stage, the TP curve also increases rapidly. Thus this stage relates to increasing returns. Here land is too much in relation to the workers employed. It is, therefore, profitable for a producer to increase workers to produce more and more output. It becomes cheaper to produce the additional output. Consequently, it would be foolish to stop producing more in this stage. Thus the producer will always expand through this stage I.

Causes of Increasing Returns

1. The main reason for increasing returns in the first stage is that in the beginning the fixed factors are larger in quantity than the variable factor. When more units of the variable factor are applied to a fixed factor, the fixed factor is used more intensively and production increases rapidly.

2. In the beginning, the fixed factor cannot be put to the maximum use due to the non applicability of sufficient units of the variable factor. But when units of the variable factor are applied in sufficient quantities, division of labour and specialization lead to per unit increase in production and the law of increasing returns operates.

3. Another reason for increasing returns is that the fixed factors are indivisible which means that they must be used in a fixed minimum size. When more units of the variable factor are applied on such a fixed factor, production increases more than proportionately. This points towards the law of increasing returns.

Stage-II : Diminishing Returns: It is the most important stage of production. Stage II starts when at point E where the MP curve intersects the AP curve which is at the maximum. Then both continue to decline with AP above MP and the TP curve begins to increase at a decreasing rate till it reaches point C. At this point the MP curve becomes negative when the TP curve begins to decline. Table 1 shows this stage when the workers are increased from 4 to 7 to cultivate the given land. In Figure 1, it lies between BE and CF. Here land is scarce and is used intensively. More and more workers are employed in order to have larger output. Thus the total product increases at a diminishing rate and the average and marginal product decline. This is the only stage in which production is feasible and profitable because in this stage the marginal productivity of labour, though positive, is diminishing but is not negative. Hence it is not correct to say that the law of variable proportions is another name for the law of diminishing returns. In fact, the law of diminishing returns is only one phase of the law of variable proportions. the law of diminishing returns in this sense has been defined by Prof. Benham thus: "As the proportion of one factor in a combination of factors is increased, after a point, the average and marginal product of that factor will diminish."

Its Causes : The Law in General Form: But the law of diminishing returns is not applicable to agriculture alone, rather it is of universal applicability. It is called the law in its general form, which states that if the proportion, in which the factors of production combin, is disturbed, the average and marginal product of that factor will diminish. The distortion in the combination of factors may be either due to the increase in the proportion of one factor in relation to others or due to the scarcity of one in relation to other factors. In either case, diseconomies of production set in, which raise costs and reduce output. For instance, if plant is expanded by installing more machines, it may become unwieldy. Entrepreneurial control and supervision become lax, and diminishing returns set in. Or, there may arise scarcity of trained labour or raw material that leads to diminution in output.

In fact, it is the scarcity of one factor in relation to other factors which is the root cause of the law of diminishing returns. The element of scarcity is found in factors because they cannot be substituted for one another. Mrs Joan Robinson explains it thus: "What the Law of Diminishing Returns really states is that there is a limelim it to the extent to which one factor of production can be substituted for another, or, in other words, that the elasticity of substitution between factors is not infinite." Suppose there is scarcity of jute, since no other fiber can be substituted for it perfectly, costs will rise with production, and diminishing returns will operate. This is because jute is not in perfectly elastic supply to the industry. If the scarce factor is rigidly fixed and it cannot be substituted by any other factor at all, diminishing returns will at once set in. If in a factory operated by electric power, there being no other substitute for it, frequent power breakdowns occur, as is commonly the case in India, production will fall and costs will rise in proportion as fixed costs will continue to be incurred even if the factory works for less hours than before.

According to Wick steed, the law of diminishing returns "is as universal as the law of life itself." The universal applicability of this law has taken economics to the realm of science.

Stage - III : Negative Marginal Returns: Production cannot take place in stage II either for in this stage, total product starts declining and the marginal product becomes negative. The employment of the 8th worker actually causes a decrease in total output from 60 to 56 units and makes the marginal product minus 4. In the figure, this stage starts from the dotted line CF where the MP curve is below the X-axis. Here the workers are too many in relation to the available land, making it absolutely impossible to cultivate it.

The Best Stage : In stage I, when production takes place to the left of point E, the fixed factor is excess in relation to the variable factors which cannot be used optimally. To the right of point F, the variable input is used excessively in Stage III. Therefore, no producer will produce in this stage because the marginal production is negative. Thus the first and third stages are of economic absurdity or economic nonsense. So production will always take place in the second stage in which total output of the firm increases at a diminishing rate and MP and AP are the maximum, then they start decreasing and production is optimum. This is the optimum and best stage of production.

5.8 Returns to Scale

Returns to scale describes the relationship between outputs and scale of inputs in the long run when all the inputs are increased in the same proportion. In the words of Prof. Roger Miller, "Returns to scale refer to the relationship between changes in output and proportionate changes in all factors of productions." To meet a long run change in demand, the firm increases its scale of production by using more space, more machines and laborers in the factory.

Assumptions

This law assumes that

1) All factors (inputs) are variable but enterprise is fixed.
2) A worker works with given tools and implements.
3) Technological changes are absent.
4) There is perfect competition.
5) The product is measured in quantities.

Explanation

Given these assumptions , when all inputs are increased in unchanged proportions and the scale of production is expanded, the effect on output three stages: increasing returns to scale, constant returns to scale and diminishing returns to scale. They are explained with the help of Table 2 and Fig. 5.

Table 2: Returns to Scale in Physical Units

Unit	Scale of Production	Total Returns	Marginal Returns	
1.	1 workers + 2 Acres Land	8	8	Increasing
2.	2 workers + 4 Acres Land	17	9	Returns
3.	3 workers + 6 Acres Land	27	10	
4.	4 workers + 8 Acres Land	38	11	Constant
5.	5 workers + 10 Acres Land	49	11	Returns
6.	6 workers + 12 Acres Land	59	10	Diminishing
7.	7 workers + 14 Acres Land	68	9	Returns
8.	8 workers + 16 Acres Land	76	8	

1. Increasing Returns to Scale

Returns to scale increase because the increase in total output is more than proportional to the increase in all inputs.

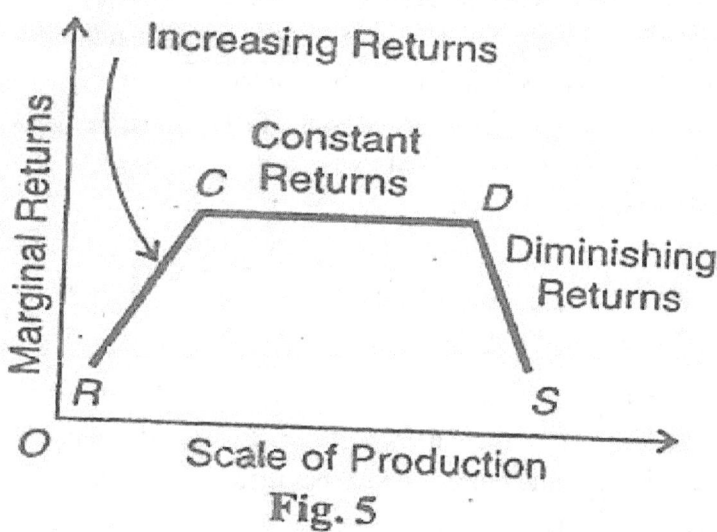

Fig. 5

The table reveals that in the beginning with the scale of production of (1 worker +2 acres of land), total output is 8. To increase output when the scale of production is doubled (2 workers + 4 acres of land), total returns are more than doubled. They become 17. Now if the scale is trebled (3 workers + 6 acres of land), returns become more than three-fold, i.e., 27. It show increasing returns to scale. In the figure RS is the returns to scale curve where R to C portion indicates increasing returns.

Causes of Increasing Returns to Scale

Returns to scale increase due to the following reasons:

(i) Indivisibility of Factors : Returns to scale increase because of the indivisibility of the factors of production. Indivisibility means that machines, management, labour, finance, etc. cannot be available in very small size. They are available in very small sizes. They are availale only in certain minimum sizes. When a business unit expands, the returns to scale increase because the indivisible factors are employed to their maximum capacity.

(ii) Specialization and Division Labour : Increasing returns to scale also result from specialization and division of labour. When the scale of the firm is expanded there is wide scope of specialization and division of labour. Work can be divided into small tasks and workers can be concentrated to to narrower range of processes. For this, specialized equipment can be installed. Thus with specialization, efficiency increases and increasing returns to scale follow.

(iii) Internal Economics: As the firm expands, it enjoys internal economies of production. It may be able to install better machines, sell its products more easily, borrow money cheaply, procure the services of more efficient manager and workers, etc. All these economies help in increasing the returns to scale more than proportionately.

(iv) External Economies: A firm also enjoys increasing returns to scale due to external economies. When the industry itself expands to meet the increased long run demand for its product, external economies appear which are shared by all the firms in the industry. When a large number of firms are concentrated at one place, skilled labour, credit and transport facilities are easily available. Subsidiary industries crop up to help the main industry. Trade journals, research and training centers appear which help in increasing the productive efficiency of the firms . Thus these external economics are also the cause of increasing returns to scale.

2. Constant Returns to Scale

Returns to scale become constant as the increase in total output is in exact proportion to the increase in inputs. If the scale of production in increased further, total returns will increase in such a way that the marginal returns become constant. In the table, for the 4 and 5 the units of the scale of production, marginal returns are 11, i.e., returns to scale are constant. In the figure, the portion from C to D of the RS curve is horizontal which depicts constant returns to scale. It means that increments of each input are constant at all levels of output.

Causes of Constant Returns to Scale

Returns to scale are constant due to:

(i) Internal Economies and Diseconomies. But increasing returns to scale do not continue indefinitely. As the firm expands further, internal economies are counterbalanced by internal diseconomies. Returns increase in the same proportion so that there are constant returns to scale over a large range of output.

(ii) External Economies and Diseconomies. The returns to scale are constant when external diseconomies and economies are neutralized and output increases in the same proportion.

(iii) Divisible Factors. When factors of production are perfectly divisible, substitutable, and homogeneous with perfectly elastic supplies at given prices, returns to scale are constant.

3. Diminishing Returns to Scale

Returns to scale diminish the increase in output is less than proportional to the increase in inputs. The table shows that when output is increased from the 6th, 7th and 8th units, the total returns increase at a lower rate than before so that the marginal returns start diminishnig successively to 10, 9 and 8. In the figure, the portion from D to S of the RS curve shows diminishing returns.

Causes of Diminishing Returns to Scale

Constant returns to scale is only a passing phase, for ultimately returns to sacel start diminishing indivisible factors may become inefficient and less productive. Business may become unwieldy and produce problems of supervision and coordination. Large management creates difficulties of control and rigidities. To theses internal diseconomies are added external diseconomies of scale. These arise from higher factor prices or from diminishing productivities of the factors. As the industry continues to expand, the demand for skilled labour, land, capital, etc. rises. There being perfect competition intensive bidding raises wages, rent and interest. Prices of raw materials also group. Transport and marketing difficulties emerge. All these factors tend to raise costs and the expansion of the firms leads t diminishing returns to scale so that doubling the scale would not lead to doubling the output.

5.9 Economies of Scale

Economies of scale, in microeconomics, refers to the cost advantages that a business obtains due to expansion. There are factors that cause a producer's average cost per unit to fall as the scale of output is increased. "Economies of scale" is a long run concept and refers to reductions in unit cost as the size of a facility and the usage levels of other inputs increase. Diseconomies of scale are the opposite. The common sources of economies of scale are purchasing (bulk buying of materials through long-term contracts), managerial (increasing the specialization of managers), financial (obtaining lower-interest charges when borrowing from banks and having access to a greater range of financial instruments), marketing (spreading the cost of advertising over a greater range of output in media markets), and technological (taking advantage of returns to scale in the production function). Each of these factors reduces the long run average costs (LRAC) of production by shifting the short-run average total cost (SRATC) curve down and to the right. Economies of scale are also derived partially from learning by doing.

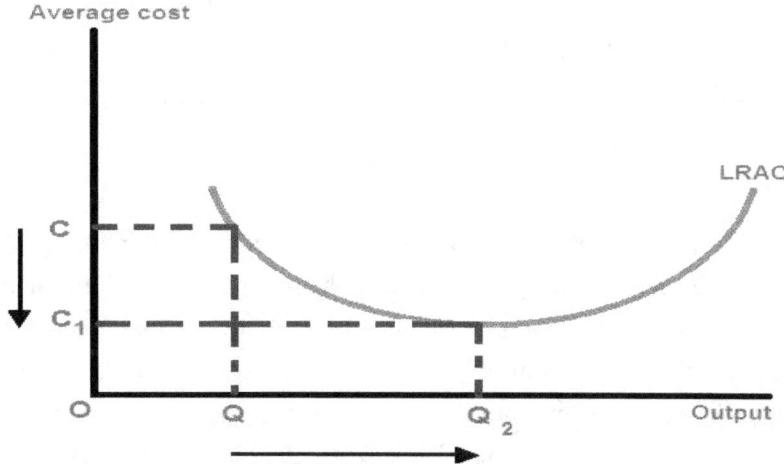

Economies of scale is a practical concept that is important for explaining real world phenomena such as patterns of international trade, the number of firms in a market, and how firms get "too big to fail".

The exploitation of economies of scale helps explain why companies grow large in some industries. It is also a justification for free trade policies, since some economies of scale may require a larger market than is possible within a particular country - for example, it would not be efficient for Liechtenstein to have its own car maker, if they would only sell to their local market. A lone car maker may be profitable, however, if they export cars to global markets in addition to selling to the local market. Economies of scale also play a role in a "natural monopoly."

An economy of scale exists when larger output is associated with lower per unit cost. Economies of scale have been classified by Marshall into Internal Economies and External Economies.

Internal Economies are internal to firm when it expands its size or increases its output. They "are open to single factory or a single firm independently of the action of other firms. They result from an increase in the scale of output of the firm, and cannot be achieved unless output increases. They are not the result of invention of any kind, but are due to the use of known methods of production which a small firm does not find worthwhile." (A.K. Cairncross)

External Economies are external to a firm which is available to it when the output of the whole industry expands. They are "shared by a number of firms or industries when the scale of production in any industry or group of industries increases. They are not monopolized by a single firm when it grows in size, but are conferred on it when some other firms grow large". (A.K. Cairncross).

Modern economists distinguish economies of scale in terms of real and pecuniary internal and external economies.

Real Internal economies are "associated with a reduction in the physical quantity of inputs, raw materials, various types of labour and various types of capital (fixed or circulating) used by a large firm."2 Real internal economies which arise from the expansion of a firm are the following:

1. **Labour Economies.** As the firm expands, it achieves labour economies with increased division of labour and specialization. When a firm expands in size, this necessitates division of labour whereby each worker is assigned one particular job, and the splitting of processes into sub-processes for greater efficiency and productivity. This, in turn, leads to the increase in the dexterity (skill) of every worker, the saving time to produce goods, and to the invention of large number of labour saving machines, according to Adam Smith. Thus division of labour and specialization lead to grather productive efficiency and reduction in per unit cost in a large firm.

2. **Technical Economies.** Technical economies are associated with all types of machines and equipments used by a large firm. They arise from the use of better machines and techniques of production which increase output and reduce per unit cost of production. Technical economies are classified as follows:

   (i) Economies of Indivisibility. Mrs. Joan Robinson refers to economies of factor indivisibility. Fixed capital is one such factor. It is indivisible in the sense that a machine, an equipment or a plant mush be used in a fixed minimum size or capacity to justify its use. Such machines can be most efficiently used at fairly large output than at small outputs because they cannot be divided into smaller units. For example, an automated car assembly plant is not a viable proposition, if the number of cars to be assembled is small because much of the plant would remain idle. But a large firm assembling a large number of cars may be able to utilise the plant to its full capacity and achieve lower per unit cost.

(ii) Economies of Superior Technique. It is only a large firm which can afford to pay for costly machines and install them. Such machines are more productive than small machines. The high cost of such machines can be spread over a larger output which they help to produce. Thus ther per unit cost of production falls in a large firm which employs costly and superior plant and equipment and thereby enjoys a technical superiority over a small firm.

(iii) Economies of Increased Dimensions. The installation of large machines itself brings may advantages to a firm. The cost of operating large machines is less than that of operating small machines. Even the cost of construction is relatively lower for large machines than for small ones. The cos of manufacture of a double-decker bus is lower as compared to the manufacture of two single-decker buses. Moreover, a double-decker carries more passengers than a single-decker and at the same time requires only a driver and a conductor like the latter. Thus its operating costs are relatively lower.

(iv) Economies of Linked Processes. A large firm is able to reduce itsper unit cost of production by linking the various processes of production. For instance, a large sugar manufacturing firm may own its sugarcane farms, manufacture sugar, pack it in bags, transport and distribute sugar through its own transport and distribution departments. Thus by linking the various processes of production and sale, a large firm saves the expenses incurred on intermediaries there by reducing unit cost of production.

(v) Economies of the Use of By-products. A large firm possesses greater rosources than a small firm and is able to utilise its waste material as a by product. For example, the molasses left over after manufacturing sugar from the surgarcane can be used for producing spirit by installing a plant for the purpose.

(vi) Economies in Power Consumption. A large firm which operates large machines and runs them continuously, economies in power consumption as compared to small machines.

3. **Marketing Economies.** A large firm also reaps the economies of buying and selling. It buys its requirements of various inputs in bulk and is, therefore, able to secure them at favorable terms in the form of better quality inputs, prompt delivery, transport concessions, etc. Because of its larger organization, it produces quality products which are offered for sale in attractive packing by its packing department. It may also have a scale department manned by experts who carry on salesmanship, propaganda and advertisement through the various media efficiently. Thus a large firm is able to reap the economies of marketing through its superior bargaining power and efficient packing and sales organization.

4. **Managerial Economies.** A large firm can afford to put specialists to supervise and manage the various departments. There may be a separate head for manufacturing, assembling, packing, marketing, general administration, etc. This decentralization leads to functional specialization which increases the productive efficiency of the firm. "Large firms apply techniques of management involving a high degree of mechanization, such as telephones, telex machines, television screens and computers. These techniques save time in decision making process and speed up to processing of information, as well as increasing its amount and its accuracy." These managerial economies also reduce per unit cost of management because with expansion of the firm, the various departmental managers will manage large output as efficiently as they were managing small output at the same salary.

5.10 Summary

Production function is an equation that asserts the relationship between the quantities of productive factors used and the maximum amount of product obtained at certain technological level. The production function can thus measure the marginal productivity of a particular factor of production and determine the cheapest combination of productive factors. Some inputs can be varied flexibly in a relatively short period of time. We conventionally think of labor and raw materials as "variable inputs" in this sense. Other inputs require a commitment over a longer period of time. We have seen that the concept of marginal productivity and the law of diminishing marginal productivity play central parts in both the efficient allocation of resources in general and in profit maximization.

5.11 Key Words

- **Production Function:** In micro-economics, A production function is a function that specifies the output of a firm, an industry, or an entire economy for all combinations of inputs.

- **Law of variable proportions:** I n economics, diminishing returns (also called diminishing marginal returns) refer to how the marginal production of a factor of production starts to progressively decrease as the factor is in creased, in contrast to the increase that would otherwise be normally expected.

- **The law of returns to scale:** An economic concept referring to a situation in which economies of scale no longer function for a firm. Rather than experiencing continued decreasing costs per increase in output, firms see an increase in marginal cost when output is increased.

- **Economies of Scale :** Economies of scale, in microeconomics, are the cost advantages that a business obtains due to expansion. They are factors that cause a producer's average cost per unit to fall as scale is in creased.

5.12 Self Assessment Test

1   What do you mean by production? Define production function and describe the assumptions.

2   What are fixed and variable inputs?

3   Distinguish between laws of return to variables proportion and laws of returns to scale

4   How will you define economy of scale?

5   What do you mean by internal and external economy of scale?

5.13 Suggested Books /References

1.   Mathur N.D., Managerial Economics, Shivam book House (P.) Limited, Jaipur

2.   Mishra & Puri : Managerial Economics, Himalaya Publishing House, Mumbai

6 Cost Concepts and Analysis

Unit Structure

6.0   Objectives

The studying this unit, you should be able to understand:

- The Concept of cost
- Different cost concepts
- Cost function
- Determinats of cost
- Components of cost

6.1   Introduction

It is necessary for the proper understanding of cost analysis, to know various cost concepts that are often employed. When an entrepreneur decides to produce a commodity, he has to pay the price for inputs which he uses in production. When he employes labour, he pays wages to them and pays money when buys raw materials, fuel and power, rent for the factory building and so on. All these are included in cost of production. The kind of cost concept used in a particular situation dependes on cost of production. The kind of cost concept used in a particular situation depends upon the business decision that the management makes. An accountant will take into account only the payments and charges made by the manager to the suppliers of various productive inputs, but the managerial economist views the cost in some what different form. The cost estimates made by contentional, financial accounting are not appropriate for all managerial uses, Further different problems call for different kinds of costs, therefore it is necessary to have a complete understanding of different cost concepts for clear business thinking.

6.2   Cost Function

Cost function is derived from the production function. Time factor is very important in cost theory. The short-run costs are the costs over a period during which some factors of production are fixed. The long-run costs are the costs over a period long enough to permit changes in all factors of production. Both in the short-run and in the long-run, cost is a multivariate function, i.e., it is determined by many factors simultaneously, symbolically, the long run cost function is given as:

$$C = f(X, T, Pf)$$

And the shot-run-run cost function is:

$$C = f(X, T, Pf, \mathbf{K})$$

Where C = Total Cost

X = Output

T = Technology

Pf = prices of factors

K = Fixed factor (s)

Graphically, the cost function is generally shown on a two-dimensional diagram by taking C= f(x), ceteris paribus, If other factors (i.e. T,Pf) to change, then the cost curve will shift.

6.3 Determinants of Costs

Factors determining the cost are

(a) Size of plant: There is an inverse relationship between size of plant and cost. As size of plant increases, cost falls and vice versa.

(b) Level of Output: There is a direct relationship between output level and cost. More the level of output, more is the cost (i. e., total cost) and vice Versa.

(c) Price of Inputs: There is a direct relationship between price of inputs and cost. As the price of inputs rises, cost ruses and vice versa.

(d) State of technology: More modern and upgraded the technology implies lesser cost and vice versa.

(e) Management and administrative efficiency: Efficiency and cost are inversely related. More the efficiency in management and administration better will be the product and less will be the cost. Cost will case of inefficiencies in management and administration.

6.4 Cost Concepts

According to Marshall, the real cost of production includes the "real cost of efforts of various Qualities" and "real cost of waiting"

It is also known as "alternative sacrificed cost, or "transfer cost". Opportunity cost of a commodity is the alternative sacrificed in order of order to order to obtain it.

Cost concepts differ because of differences in view point. Different combinations of cost ingredients are important for various kinds of management problems. Disparities occur form deletions, from additions from recombination which do not appear anywhere in the accounting records. Different cost concepts explained in our study are

(a) Actual cost and opportunity costs

(b) Past and future costs

(c) Short run and long run costs

(d) Variable or Prime cost and fixed costs or supplementary costs

(e)   Incremental costs and sunk costs

(f)   Traceable and Non-Traceable costs

(g)   Explicit and Implicit costs

(h)   Controllable and Non-Controllable Costs

(i)   Private, External and social costs

(j)   Total. Average and Marginal Costs

(a) Actual Cost and Opportunity Cost

Actual costs are those that involve financial expenditure incurred for acquiring inputs for producing a commodity. These expenditures are recorded in the books of accounts of the firm. The expenditures are wages, payment made for the purchase made for the purchase of raw materials machinery etc. These costs are called actual costs or outlay costs or real costs. The real cost of production has been interpreted in different forms. According to Adam Smith, "Pains and sacrifices of labour are real cost of production" Opportunity cost is not the actual expenditure but it is the revenue earned by employing that good or service in some other alternative uses. Opportunity cost is the cost of producing any commodity in the next best alternative cost. For example the inputs which are used to manufacture a car may also be used in the productions of military equipment. A farmer who is producing paddy can also produce sugar cane with the same factors. Therefore, the opportunity cost of one quintal of paddy is the amount of sugarcane given up. Main points of opportunity cost are:

1.   The opportunity cost of any commodity is only the next best alternative forgone.

2.   The next best alternative commodity that could be produced with the same value of the factors, which are more or less the same.

3.   It helps in determining relative prices of factor inputs at different places.

4.   It helps in determining the remuneration to services.

5.   It helps the manager to decide what he should produce in the factory.

(b) Past and Future Costs

Past costs are actual costs incurred in the past. These costs are mentioned in the financial accounts. Future costs are those costs which are to be incurred in the near future. This is only a forecast. Future costs matter for managerial decisions because, the management can evaluate the desirability of that expenditure, since the past costs are costs that have already been incurred, and there is no scope for managerial decision. If the management finds out that the past costs are excessive, it cannot do anything to rectify it now. In the case of future costs, if the management considers them very high , it can either reduce them or postpone the use of them.

(c) sort Run and Long Run Costs

Shorts run costs are those associated with variation in the utilization of fixed plan or other facilities, whereas long run costs encompass changes in the size and kind of plant. Short run cost is relevant when a firm has to decide whether or not to produce more or less with the given plant and equipments. If the firm dicides to expand the capacity of the plant, it must examine the long run cost. Long run cost is useful in making investment decisions.

(d) Prime or Variable Costs and Supplementary or Fixed Costs

Prime costs are variable or direct costs. Normally, they include the money cost of the raw material used in making a commodity, the wages of the labour directly spent on it and the extra wear and tear of the machine that makes it. Suppose a carpenter has been asked to charge for a chair, he would first think of the wood and cane that he used and the number of days he spent in making it. This is the prime cost.

It is clear that prime cost of a commodity differs with the quantity produced. When more chairs are made, more money will have to be spent on carpenter's wages as well as on wood. When production is stopped, the prime costs disappear. Prime costs therefore are also called the Variable Costs.

Supplementary or Fixed Costs

The carpenter will not only charge for the chair but also for the wood and his wage. In addition to the above he will think of including a portion of rent in the cost that he is paying and also interest on the capital invested, the municipal taxes, etc. A big company will further have to include a portion of the salaries of the manager, the peons, the cost of advertisement and salesmanship, etc. These costs must also be covered. They are called supplementary costs on costs or over head charges or fixed costs.

The fixed costs do not change with the volume of production. Irrespective of quantity of goods produced, big or small, the charges on account of rent, taxes, interest salaries, etc will be included. Even if the orders cease to flow in and the factory is closed, these costs will continue. They are fixed costs.

Generally, the distinction between the variable and fixed costs applies only to the short period, because nothing can really remain fixed in the long run. In the long the strength and the salary bill of the staff may change, the amount of capital invested may be different, hence the amount of interest would vary. Thus, all costs, which ware regarded as fixed in the short run, may vary in the long run. Thus in the long run, all costs are variable.

(e) Incremental Costs and Sunk Costs

Incremental costs are the added costs of a change in the level of production or the nature of activity. It may be adding a new product or changing distribution channel, or adding new machinery, etc. It appears to be similar to marginal cost, but it is not managerial cost. Marginal cost refers to the cost on added unit of output.

Sunk costs are costs which cannot be altered in any way. Sunk costs are costs which have already been uncured. For example, cost incurred in constructing a factory. When the factory building is constructed costs have already been incurred. The building has to be used for which originally envisaged. It cannot be altered when operations are increased or decreased. Investment on machinery is an example of sunk cost.

The distinction between the sunk cost and the incremental cost is important in evaluating the alterative. Incremental cost will be different in the case of different alternative. Hence incremental cost is relevant for the management in decision making. Sunk cost will remain the same irrespective or the alternative in decision making. Sunk cost will remain the same irrespective of the alternative selected. Marketing programme has its own set of incremental costs for equipment, delivery men and executive time and so on.

(f) Traceable Costs and Non-traceable Costs

Traceable costs are those which can easily be identified by a producing unit. These are directly related to a unit of operation like a product, a process or department of firm. These are also know as direct costs or assignable costs.

Non-traceable costs or indirect costs are not traceable to plant, department or unit or operation or individual final product. Fox example, for operating air-services, the cost of runway, airport equipment, staff, etc. cannot be assigned to one passenger. These are common costs to distinguish between traceable and non-traceable costs. Change in the total output and product-mix affect the total costs in complex ways. Even a traceable cost gets lost in the process and has to be indentified as overhead cost only.

(g) Explicit Cost and Implicit Costs

The total cost of production of a particular commodity can be said to include 'Expenditure' or 'explicit' cost, 'non-expenditure' or 'implicit' cost. Explicit costs are paid by the employer to owners of the factor units, which do not belong to the employer himself. These costs include payments for raw materials interest on borrowed funds, rent on hired land and taxes paid to the government.

Non-expenditure or implicit costs arise when factor units are owned by the employer himself, The two non expenditure costs are supplied by the shareholders; in the case of small business units the depreciation and an average or normal return on the money capital wages of the entrepreneur or organizer himself will have to be included in this category.

Expenditure costs are explicit since they are paid to factors outside the firm while non-expenditure costs are implicit and hence they are imputed costs.

(h) Controllable Costs and Non-Controllable costs

Controllable costs are those that cannot be controlled by some executive action on the part of the management These can improve the efficiency of the factor inputs.

Non-controllable costs are those that cannot be controlled through any administrative or supervisory action. These tend to wastage of resources and encourage inefficiency.

(i) Private, External and Social Costs

Some times, there is a discrepancy between the cost incurred by a firm and the cost that must be incurred by the society as a whole. For example, a factory may dispose of its untreated waste into a river or a lake. Such a method of waste disposal may minimize the private cost but it does impose a cost to the society in the form of polluted waterways. A cost that is not borne by the firm, but is incurred by others in society is called an external cost. The true cost to the society must include all costs regardless of who bears them. Thus, the social cost is the sum of private and external cost. This is

Social cost = Private Cost + External Cost

Or

External Cost = Social Cost - Private Cost

(j) Total, Average and Marginal Costs

Total cost is made up of both the fixed cost and the variable cost. They are represented in the following diagram. OX and OY are the two axes, along OX is represented the quantity produced and along OY the cost. FC, a straight horizontal line represents the fixed cost and the area above is the variable cost so that the TC is total cost curve.

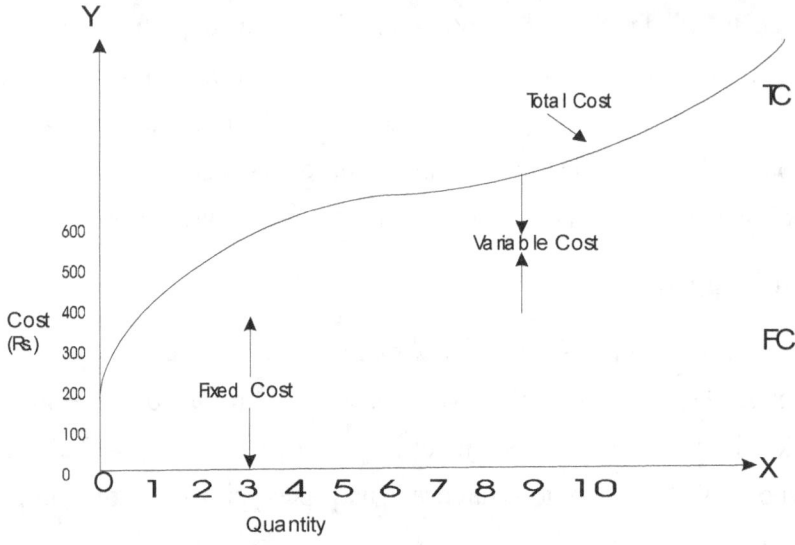

Fixed Cost, Variable Cost, Total Cost Curves

$$\text{Average cost at any output} = \frac{\text{Total Cost}}{\text{Units of output}}$$

Average Cost: Average cost is the sum of average variable cost and average fixed cost; it is also called average total cost. If the totalcost of producing 60 units of good is 2400 rupees, then average cost.will be

$$\frac{2400}{120} = 20$$

Marginal Cost : Marginal cost is the cost of producing an additional unit of output. In other words, marginal cost is the addition made to the total cost by producing one more unit of output. for example, if the total cost of producing 120 units is 2400 rupees and the total cost of producing 121 units is 2436 rupees, the marginal costing in this case will be equal to 36 rupees.The concepts of total cost, average cost and marginal cost can be understood easily form the following table;

Total, Average and Marginal Costs

Output	Total Cost	Average Cost	Marginal cost
	Rs.	Rs.	Rs.
1.	60	60	60
2.	80	40	20
3.	90	30	10
4.	96	24	6
5.	100	20	4
6.	144	24	44
7.	210	30	66
8.	320	40	110
9.	540	60	220
10.	900	90	360

It is evident from the above table that marginal cost of the second unit has been derived from subtracting Rs60 from Rs80 (80-60) =20. Marginal costs of subsequent units are obtained in the same manner. Hence Marginal cost is the addition made to the total cost at each step.

Marginal Cost and Average Cost

Generally, the average and marginal costs are related together. It is evident from the above table that when the average cost is falling, the marginal cost is less than the average cost and when average cost is rising, the marginal cost is higher than the average cost. When the marginal cost neither goes up nor comes down, the average and marginal cost are equal. In the table, up to 5th unit average cost is falling. It will be seen from the fourth column that from 6th to 10th unit average cost is rising. It will be seen from the table that marginal cost is higher than average cost in this range.

For instance, let us assume that a cricket player's batting average is 50. suppose, in the next match, he scor less than 50, say 45, his batting average will decrease, because his additional (i.e. marginal) scores (45) is less than his average score (50). Suppose, on the other hand in the next match, he scores more than the average (50), say 60, his average will go up for the obvious reason that this new or additional (i.e., marginal score 60) is higher than his average score (50) thus, when the marginal is rising, the average goes up, and if the marginal is falling, the average goes down. When, however, the marginal remains unchanged, the average and marginal are equal.

The following diagram show the average – marginal cost relationship:

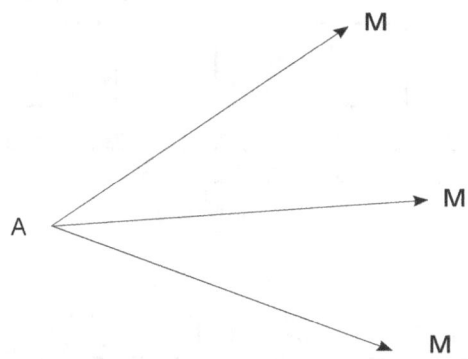

In the above figure, A represents the average cost and M represents the marginal cost. It can be clearly seen that when marginal cost (M) is above the average cost (A), the average cost rises which is shown by the rising arrow. On the other hand, when the marginal (M) is below the average cost (A), than the average cost falls, as is shown by the falling arrow. But when the marginal cost is the same as the average cost remains constant, as if M is pulling A along horizontally.

Curve can be drawn to represent costs. The marginal cost (MC) and the average cost (AC) are shown in the following diagram.

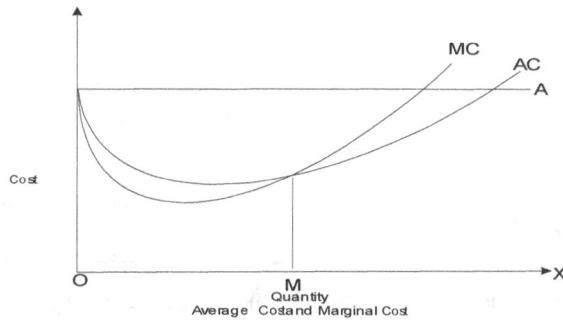

Average Cost and Marginal Cost

OX and OY are two axes, along OX is shown the quantity produced and along OY the cost. It will be seen that as output is increased, both average cost (AC) and marginal cost (MC) fall, but MC is below AC, i.e., marginal cost is less than the average cost. The fall is due to the economics of scale. But beyond a point (M) i.e. when output is expanded too much, both AC and MC start rising and now MC is above AC, i.e., the marginal cost is greater than the average cost. That is why MC cuts AC from below at its lowest point.

67

6.5 Components of Costs

Classification of total cost on the basis of the cost fixed and variable inputs is not enough for taking managerial decisions. A firm has to work out in detail the different expenses that it incurs on various heads. In order to compute profit and loss a form has to analyse the 'components' or 'elements' of total cost.

Functionally, the major components of the total cost of a product the comprises the total costs can be divided as follows:

(i) Prime Cost = Direct Material + Direct Wages + Direct Expenses

(ii) Production Overhead = Indirect Material + Indirect Wages + Indirect Expenses

(iii) Production cost = Prime Cost + Production overhead

(iv) Costs Related to = General Administration = Marketing/Sales = Research = Development

(v) Total = Production Cost + Costs Related to other functions

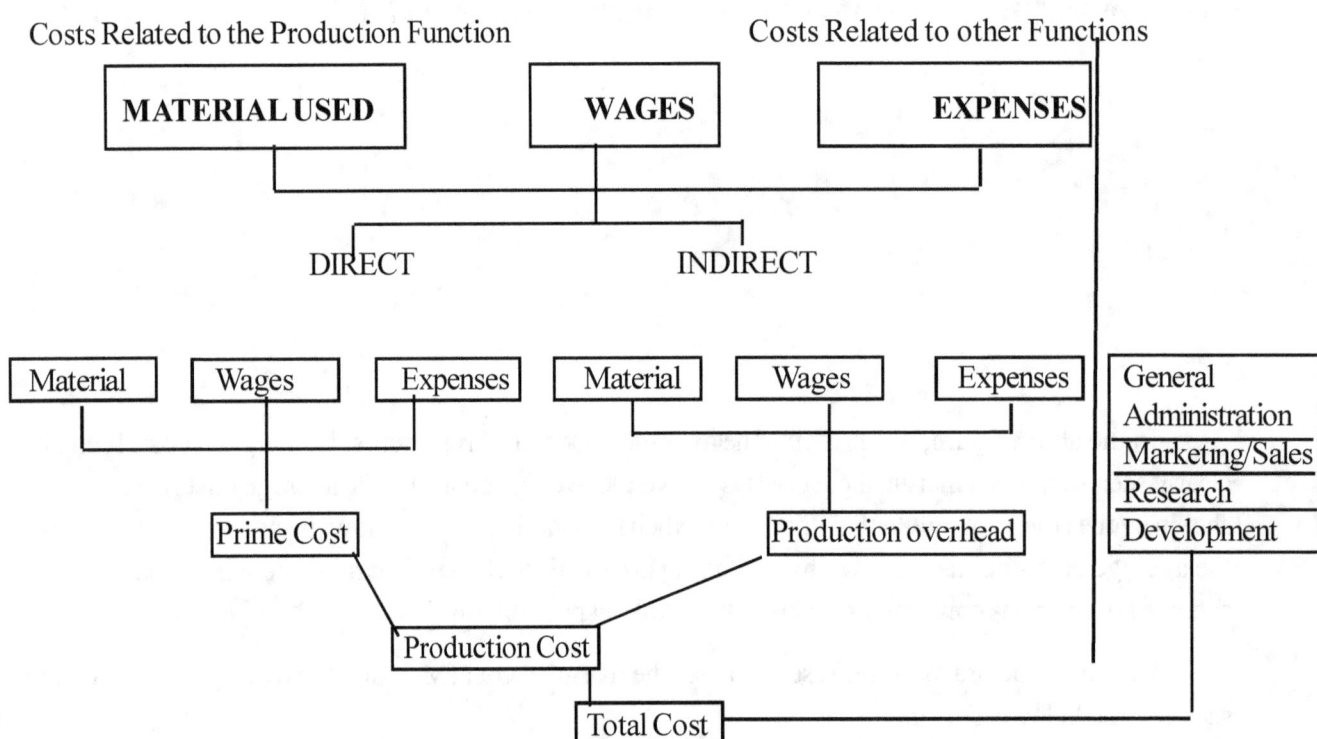

The difference between total revenue and total cost revenue and total cost represents profits or loss. In case, the TR is move than the cost of sales the firm gets profit, while if TR is less than the cost of sales the firm suffers loss.

6.6 Short Run Cost Function

The short-run refers to that period of time within which a firm can vary its output by varying only the amount of variable factors, factors such as labour and raw material. In the short run period the firm cannot alter the fixed factors such capital equipment management personal, the factory buildings etc. Suppose a firm wants to increase production in the short run it can do so only by hiring more worker or buying and using more raw materials. In the short run a firm cannot enlarge the size of the existing plant or build a new plant of a bigger capacity. Thus in the short run only variable factors can be varied while the fixed factors remain the same.

Short-run Fixed and Variable Costs

In the period, the prime costs relating to lobour and raw material can be varied whereas the fixed costs remain the same. On the other hand, in the long period, even the fixed costs relating to plant and machinery, staff salaries, etc, can be varied. That is, in the long run all costs are variable and no costs are fixed.

Short-run Cost Curve

Generally, in the short-run a firm will adjust output to demand by varying the variable factors. When the factors of production can be used in varying proportions, it means that the scale of operations of the firm can be changed. Each time the scale of operations is changed, a new short-run curve will have to be drawn for the firm such as SAC' SAC" and SAC" in the next.

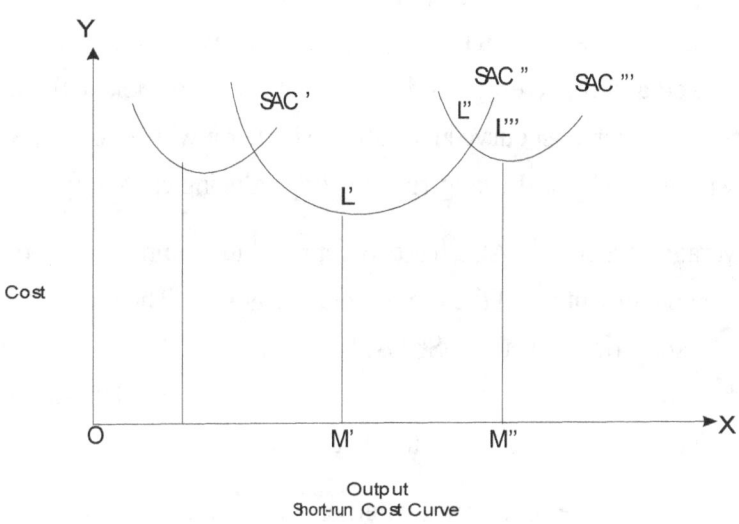

Output
Short-run Cost Curve

Suppose, a firm has the short-run cost curve SAV". In this case, the optimum will be OM'. When it wants to increase the output to OM" in the short-run it can be obtained at the average cost M"L" along the short-run cost curve Sac:, because in the short-run the scale of operation is fixed.

On the other hand, during the long run, a new and bigger plant can be built on which OM" is the optimum output. That is, the firm has now a short run average cost curve SAC", and by increasing the scale of its operations, the firm can produce the OM" output at a cost of M"L" instead of M"L".

It is evident form the above figure that at any scale of operations in the short-run, a firm will have regions of rising and falling costs. On the other hand, in the long-run the firm can produce on a completely short-run cost curve, and there will be an output where the average cost is minimum. This is the optimum output.

6.7 Long-Run Average Cost Curve

In the following diagram SAC', SAC" and SAC"' refer to the short run cost curve corresponding to the different scales of operations. In the following situations the firm will be producing the desired output at the lowest cost. For example. OM output is produced at PM in the scale of operations represented by the curve SAC. OM will be produced on SAC, and so on.

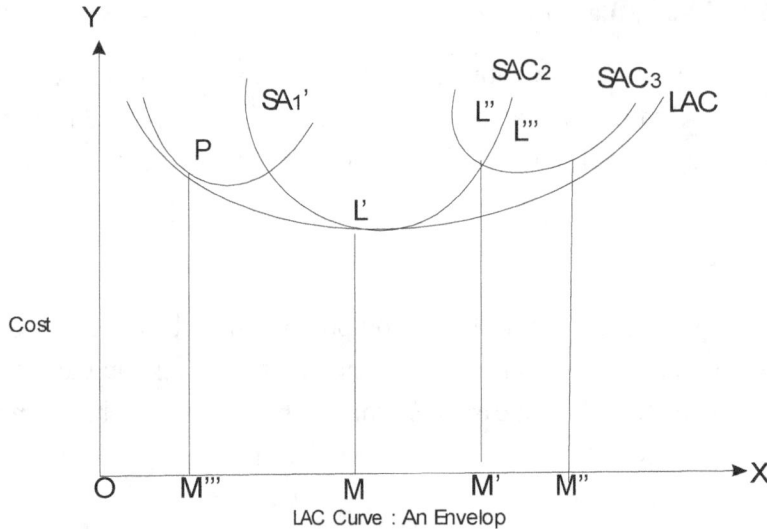

LAC Curve : An Envelop

However, it is imperative that only in the long-run the scale of operations can be altered; in the short-run, in it will be fixed and the average cost of output above of below the optimum level will necessarily rise along the short-run cost curve in question whether it will be SAC1, SAC2 and SAC3. A long run average cost will show what is the long-run cost of producing each output.

The short-run average cost curve SAC2 has a lower minimum point that either the curves SAC1, SAC2 and SAC3. The maximum output of the firm is obtained at OM. The long-run average cost curve LAC is a tangent to all the short run cost curve. SAC1, SAC2 and SAC3. The LAC curve will therefore, be U-shaped like the short-run cost curve. It will be flatter. That is why the long-run cost curve is called an 'Envelope' , because it envelops all the short-run cost curves.

According to Dewett and Varma, the cost curve, whether short-run or long-run are U-shaped because the cost of production first starts falling as output is increased owing to the various economies of scale. But after touching the lowest point at the optimum output level, it starts rising, and goes on rising if production is continued beyond the optimum level. This obviously makes a U-shape.

The U-shape of the long-run cost curves is less pronounced. In other words, the long run average costs are than the short-run curves. The longer the period to which the curve relates the less pronounced will be the U-shape of the curve. By the long period the size and organization of the firm can be altered to meet the changed conditions.

6.8 Summary

For clear business decisions it is necessary to have complete understanding of different cost concepts. For proper knowledge of cost analysis, various cost concepts include and determine cost of production which enables management for correct business decisions. Various combinations of costs ingredients account for various kind of management decisions.

In short period, the price cost relating to labour and raw material can be varied whereas fixed cost remains the same. On the other hand in long period even fixed cost relating to plant & machinery staff salaries can be varied or in other words in long run all costs are variable.

For Completing profit & loss a firm has to analyse the components or elements of total costs.

6.9 Key Words

- **Short run cost:** Cost over a period during which some factors of production are fixed.

- **Long run cost:** Cost over a long period to permit changes in all factors of production.

- **Post costs:** Actual costs incurred in the past.

- **Future costs:** Which are to be incurred in near future.

- **Prime costs:** Refers to variable or direct costs.

- **Incremental cost:** Added cost of a change in the level of production.

- **Sunk cost:** Which have all ready been incurred and cannot be altered.

- **Traceable cost:** Which are easily be identified by a producing unit.

- **Non Traceable cost:** Which are not traceable to plant, department of unit of operation.

- **Explicit cost & inexplicit cost:** Total cost of production of a commodity can be said to include expenditure explicit cost and non expenditure or inexplicit cost.

- **Controllable cost:** That can be controlled by some executive action in the part of management.

- **Non Controllable cost:** That can not be controlled through any administrative or supervisory action.

- **Total Cost:** Made up of both fixed and variable cost.

- **Average Cost:** Product of total cost to units of output or sum of average variable cost and fixed cost.

6.9 Self Assessment Test

1. Discuss briefly the different cost concepts.

2. Explain the determinants of costs.

3. Distingusish between:
   (a) Fixed and variable cost
   (b) Average and implicit cost
   (c) Explicit and Implicit cost

4. Firm plans in long run and operate in short run. Explain.

6.11 Suggested Books/References

1. Mathur N.D.: Managerial Economics, Shivam Books House (P.) Limited, Jaipur

2 Adhikari M.: Managerial Economics, Khosla Educational Publisher, New Delhi.

7 Market Structure

Unit Structure

7.0   Objectives

After studying this unit, you should be able to understand:

- The concept of market
- The saliant features of market
- Classification of market
- Concept of market structure
- Types of market structure
- The issues in market structure

7.1   Introduction

In general, market means a place where there are many buyers and sellers of different products who are actively engaged in buying and selling acts. The firm's demand curve is expected to depend on such things as the numbers of sellers in the market and the similarity of their products. These are the aspects of market structure which may be termed as the characteristics of market of generalisation that are likely to influence a firm's behaviour and performance. In broader sense face to face contact between buyers and sellers is not necessary. They can establish contact through different means of communication like letters, agents, telegraphs, telephone etc. or newspapers. Thus, the terms market does not mean and particular place but the entire area where buyers and sellers of a commodity are in such close contact with each other that the price of the same commodity tends to be one throughout that area.

According to Cournot, "Economists understand by the term market not any particular market place in which things are bought and sold but the whole of any region in which buyers and sellers are in such free intercourse with each other that the price of the same goods tends to uniformity, easily and quickly."

According to J.C. Edwards, "A market is that mechanism by which buyers and sellers are brought together. It is not necessarily a fixed place."

Chapman defines as "The term market refers not necessarily to place but always to a commodity and the buyers and sellers who are in direct competition with one another."

7.2 Objective of Market Structure

Market Structure influences how a firm behaves in pricing, supply, barrier of entry, efficiency, competition.

- It enables an organisation to control its market plan.

- Market Structure helps in strategic decision making.

- Market Structure aligns the organisation to the changed environment.

- Market Structure is important and it affects market outcomes through its impact on motivation, opportunities & decision of economic factors.

On the basis of above mentioned definition following characteristics can be brought out:

1- Area: Market does not mean any particular place where buyers and sellers meet, rather, it means the entire area within which buyers and sellers are spread and have close contacts with each other. For example Bata Shoes has market all over India., because its buyers and sellers are found in every city and state.

2- Buyers & Sellers: For exchange at least one buyer and one seller are needed. Thus, the existence of buyers and sellers is a must. If one of the two does not exist in a region, it does not satisfy the function of market. It is not necessary that buyers and sellers should be physically present to exchange or transact the things. They can come in contact through correspondence.

3- One Commodity: For the existence of the market there must be one commodity like wheat, sugar, ghee, vegetables and utensils. Thus they can be termed as wheat market, sugar market, ghee market, vegetables market, utensils market respectively.

4- Free Competition: There must be healthy and free competition among the buyers and sellers. Thus in practice, there should not be any restrictions on them. There must be free competition.

5- One Price: Generally it is remarked that in a market one price prevails which is the main feature and testimony of a market.

7.3 Classification of Market

(1) On the basis of area or region:

The economists have classified the market on the basis of area or region which further can be summarised as under.

(i) Local Market
(ii) Regional or Provincial Market
(iii) National Market
(iv) International Market

(i) Local Market: If the buyers and sellers of a certain commodity are limited to certain area or region, then it is called local market. The perishable goods and low price goods have their local market like milk, ghee, hand-made fans, basket, cots etc.

(ii) Regional or Provincial Market: If the buyers and sellers of a commodity are confined to certain region, say a province like Rajasthan or Haryana, then it is known as regional or provincial market. The area of regional market is greater than that of local market e.g. the demand for Red Bangles in Rajasthan or the demand for Laharia in Rajasthan.

(iii) National Market: When the buyers and sellers are not confined to state boundary, but are spread throughout the country e.g., the market of sarees and dhotis or of Gandhian cap or of Nehru cut jacket etc. have national market. These are demanded throughout the nation. Hence they come under the purview of national market.

(iv) International Market: When the buyers and sellers are spread across the geographical boundary of a nation and the demand for such product is worldwide or universal demand then its market is known as international market e.g. market for gold and silver.

(2) On the basis of time:

On the basis of time the economist have classified the market as under:

(i) Very short period Market.
(ii) Short period Market.
(iii) Long period Market.
(iv) Very long period Market.

(i) Very short period Market: This market can further be classified into Daily Market or Weekly market. Very short period market is that market which takes part in transaction for a very short period of time say a few hours a day or so. In very short period the supply of the product cannot be increased e.g. of milk. Here the demand determines the price. In very short period market generally perishable commodities are exchanged.

Daily Market- The market for perishable commodities come under daily market e.g. milk and vegetables.

Weekly Market- Sometimes a market operates on any specific day of week. It is generally found in those areas in which main market has its closed day for the week, say Sunday market, or Tuesday market or whatever the case may be according to the closing day of the main market.

(ii) Short period Market: Its time period is greater than that of the previous one in which the supply of the product can be increased but we cannot make any change in production plant according to the changed demand. In short period also the demand side plays a major role in determining the price as change in the plant and machinery is not possible from the point of view of production.

(iii) Long Period Market: It is such a market in which we can make necessary changes in the plant and machinery as well to increase the supply of the product according to its demand. The supply of the product plays a vital role in price determination resulting in normal price for the product in such market.

(iv) Very long period Market: There can be an enormous change in the supply of the product in very long period market. New techniques of production, innovations and the new models of products can be produced because of a very long period. And in very long periods the demand also increases because of change in population, habits, customs, fashions etc.

(3) On the basis of Functions:

On the basis of functions the markets can be classified as under:

(i) Mixed or general Market.
(ii) Specialised Market
(iii) Marketing by samples.
(iv) Marketing by grading.

(i) Mixed or general Market: When different types of commodities are transacted simultaneously in a market then it is known as mixed or general market e.g. Chandni Chowk market in Delhi.

(ii) Specialised Market: When only one product or any of the special product is transacted in a market then it is known as specialised market. In such market, a particular thing is traded with its different brand names of possibly different kinds, e.g. bathing soap is bought and sold in soap market could be Lux, Liril, Hamam, Rexona, Lifebuoy, etc.

(iii) Marketing by Samples: In such market the firms need not show whole of their product. They only send samples through their agents or they may themselves show the samples of their product, e.g. in case of wool, cloth, paints etc.

(iv) Marketing by Grading: The product is first graded according to its quality and then put forth for selling is known as marketing by grading e.g. in an Agricultural product market the product is graded accordingly and then sold. It is known as Marketing by grading.

(4) On the basis of nature of commodity:

The market can also be classified on the basis of nature of commodity.

(i) Product Market.
(ii) Stock Market.
(iii) Bullion Market.

(i) Product Market: The production goods are exchanged in these market e.g. Agriculture product is bought and sold in Agriculture produce market.

(ii) Stock Market: Stock market is a market where stock and shares, bonds, securities, debentures etc. are bought and sold. Bulls and Bears do transactions in the stock market as per their market reading.

(iii) Bullion Market: This is such a market in which Metallic trading exists e.g. the goods like silver and gold better known as Bullion are traded and transacted.

(5) On the basis of Legality:

On the basis the market can be sub-divided as under:

(i) Legal or fair Market.
(ii) Illegal Market.

(i) Legal and Fair Market: When the goods are transacted in a market under certain norms and rules, the market is known as legal market which also has a legal sanctity behind it issued by the legal authorities in a country. Here every consumer gets commodities at fair prices. These markets are also known as Fair Market.

(ii) Illegal Market: When the transaction of certain commodities is taking place in more than or less than quantity prescribed by the legal authorities in operation say a government and then it is termed as illegal trade. The Hong Kong Market is an illegal market at International level. Generally it is also termed as Chor Market.

CLASSIFICATION OF MARKET

The economists have classified the market on the basis of following elements.

General classification of market

S.No.	On the basis of Area or Region	On the basis of Time	On the basis of Functions	On the basis of nature of commodity	On the basis of legality
1-	Local Market	Very short period market	Mixed market or general market	Product market	Legal market
2-	Regional Market or Provincial market	Short period market	Specialised market	Stock market	Illegal market
3-	National market	Long period market	Marketing by sample	Bullion market	--
4-	International market	Very long period market	Marking by grades	Bullion market	--

7.4 Market Structure

The level of production of any commodity depends upon structure of its market. Possible outcomes of sales, revenues, profits are prices and structured under market structures. The firms demand curve to the industry demand curve is expected to depend on such things as the number of sellers in the market and the similarity of their products. These are aspects of market structures which may be called characteristics of market or generalization that are likely to influence firm's behaviour and performance. There are many other aspects of market structure that may influence behaviour. These include the ease of entering the industry, the nature and size of the purchasers of the firm's products, and the firms ability to influence demand by advertising. To reduce the discussion to manageable size, economists have focused on a few theoretical market structures that are expected to represent a high proportion of the cases actually encountered market societies. In this portion we shall look at four of these : Perfect competition, Monopoly, Monopolistic competition and Oligopoly.

The price and level of production of a commodity depends upon the market structure of its conditions. Market demand depends on the following factors :

(i)   Nature of the commodity : It is to be taken into account whether the goods are homogeneous or heterogeneous.

(ii) Number of buyers and sellers of the product in the market.

(iii) Mutual inter-dependence of buyers and sellers.

In brief the market structure depends on the level or forms of competition which are as under:

(1) Perfect Competition

(2) Monopoly

(3) Imperfect Competition

PERFECT COMPETITION:

It is such a market structure where there are large number of buyers and sellers of a homogeneous product and the price of the product is determined by the industry. There is one price that prevails in the market. All firms sell the product at the prevailing price.

According to Leftwitch, "Perfect competition is a market in which there are many firms selling identical product with no firm being large enough relative to the entire market so as to be able to influence market price."

In other words a perfectly competitive firm is too small and insignificant to affect the market price like a wheat farmer. He is a price taker who can sell all he wishes to sell at the ruling market price. In terms of elasticity of demand a perfect competitor faces a horizontal demand curve (parallel to the X-axis) for his product, coefficient of elasticity being infinite.

The main characteristics of perfect competition are as follows:

(1) Large number of buyers and sellers: There is a large number of buyers and sellers of a commodity under perfect competition but each buyer and each seller is so small in comparison with entire market of product that he cannot influence the market price by changing the quantity of the product sold by him. If a seller supplies the entire stock of the product produced by him the total supply will not increase to such as extent as to lower the price and on the other hand if he withdraws from the market the total supply will not fall to such an extent as to raise the price. Thus, every seller has to accept the prevailing price. Hence a uniformity of price is there under perfect competition and as a consequence of uniform price prevailing in the market average revenue (AR) or the price of the product is equal to the marginal revenue (MR) as shown in diagram .7. Average revenue is total sales proceeds of the product divided by the total production.

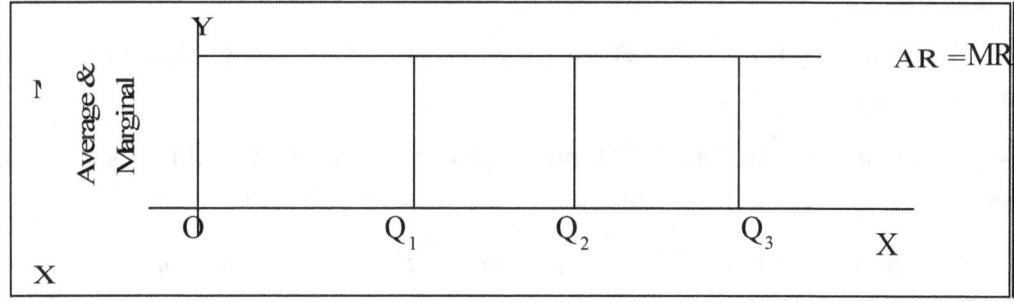

Diagram 7.1

(2) Homogeneous Product: The second important charactristic of the perfectly competitive market is that the product sold by the various firms are homogeneous. The products are homogenous in the sense that they are perfect substitutes from the buyer's point of view. The sellers do not spend on advertisement and publicity etc. because all the firms sell homogeneous product.

(3) Absence of artificial Restrictions: The third major characteristic of the perfect competition is the non-existence of any artificial restrictions on the demands, supplies, prices of goods and factors of productions in the market. There must not be any external intervention in price fixation and any controls on the product.

(4) Free entry and exit: The fourth characteristic of perfect competition is free entry and free exit for the firms under perfectly competitive market. The firms are free to enter or to exit from the industry whenever they want to do so. Any firm can enter or leave the industry at any time as there are no legal restrictions.

77

(5) Perfect knowledge about the market: There is perfect knowledge on the part of buyers and sellers about market conditions. The buyers and sellers are fully aware of the price prevailing in the market. Due to this awareness all the firms charge on price from the buyers.

(6) Perfect mobility of the factors of production: The existence of perfect mobility of the factors of production is another important characteristic of the perfect competition for its smooth functioning. It means all the factors of production are perfectly mobile under perfectly competitive market. Factors will move to the industry which pays the higher remuneration.

(7) Non-Existence of transportation cost: A perfectly competitive market also assumes the characteristic of non-existence of transport costs as uniform price prevails throughout the market. It is essential that there is no transportation cost across different areas of the market. Thus, the existence of a single uniform price is an essential feature of a perfectly competitive market and a single uniform price for the same product cannot exist in the market if transportation costs are taken into accounts.

MONOPOLY:

It is a market structure in which there is only a single seller of the product. Here one firm is selling the product and has full control over the supply of the product e.g. the supply of electricity by the Rajasthan State Electricity Board or postage stamps, post cards, envelopes Indian Postal Orders etc. are supplied by the Postal Dept. This is such a situation of market where, there is only one producer of a commodity with no close substitutes. Hence, monopoly is a market structure in which there is only one producer of a commodity with no close substitute. Thus, the analysis of monopoly begins with two simple assumptions:

(i) First, that an entire industry in supplied by a single seller who is called a monopolist;

(ii) Second by the monopolist sets a single price and supplies all buyers who wish to buy at that price.

According to Ferguson, "A pure monopoly exists when there is only one producer in a market. There are no direct competitors."

According to A. Koutsoyiannis, "Monopoly is a market situation in which there is a single seller, there are no close substitutes for commodity it produces, there are barriers to entry."

For the smooth functioning of a monopoly market situation it is necessary to have the following characteristics or features.

1. Sole supplier of the product and large number of buyers: The monopoly is characterised by the sole seller of product in an industry. Firm represents the industry as a whole which has complete control over the supply of product. Thus, there is only one firm under monopoly but the buyers of the product are in large number, consequently, no buyer can influence the price of the product.

2. No close substitutes: Under Monopoly there are no close substitutes of the product. Monopoly cannot continue if there is availability of substitute goods.

3. One firm industry: There being only one firm, the distinction between the firm and the industry is no longer in existence.

4. Monopoly may vary from industry to industry: The form and structure of a monopoly may also vary from industry to industry.

5. Absence of Entry: Under monopoly market structure no other firm can enter the market. It implies the absence of actual entry. The barriers to the entry may be artificial, legal, natural, economic and institutional etc.

6. Monopolist is a Price maker: Under Monopoly, market structure is a price maker not the price taker because of the fact that a monopolist has full control over the supply of the commodity. The fortunate monopolist can fix whatever price he chooses. But if his sale is not enough, then he may lose instead of gaining.

After discussing monopoly we may note certain other forms which are offshoot of monopoly. They are (i) MONOPSONY, (2) BILATERAL MONOPOLY. In monopsony there is only one buyer but there are large number of sellers. Price is determined by negotiation and output is determined on the basis of orders placed by the buyer. In bilateral monopoly there is one buyer and only one seller of the commodity.

IMPERFECT COMPETITION:

The market structure may be imperfect because of the number of firms in the industry may be relatively small, and the commodity or service may not be homogeneous. A small number of firms may compete vigorously with one another. Thus, in real life, it is imperfect by competitive market that exists. The concept of imperfect competition was developed in 1933 by Mrs. Joan Robinson and Prof. Chamberlin. It is such a market structure where there are many sellers of the products, but the product of each seller is different from the product of other sellers. This product differentiation manifests itself in trade mark, name of the brand, patent, rights, colour composition of goods, chemical composition, packaging, advertising, incentive schemes, or different facilities and services offered to the consumers. Thus, imperfect competition can be of various types as follows:

(1) Monopolistic Competition
(2) Oligopoly
(3) Duopoly

(1) MONOPOLISTIC COMPETITION:

As a matter of fact, monopolistic competition is a mid-way between perfect competition and monopoly. Under perfect competition the number of sellers is very large and unlimited and under monopoly there is only single seller of the product, while under monopolistic competition the number of sellers is relatively limited.

Some main definitions of monopolistic competition are as follows:

According to J.S. Bain, "Monopolistic competition is a market structure found in the industry where there are large number of small sellers, selling differentiated but close substitute products."

According to Lim Chungyoh, "Monopolistic competition is a market situation where there are many producers but each offers a slightly differentiated product."

(1) Large number of firms: There is a large number of firms or sellers operating under monopolistic competition but a relatively small fraction of the total market is shared by each firm or seller.

(2) Product differentiation: The second distinct feature of monopolistic competitive market structure is product differentiation. The number of firms is large but their products differ from one another in colours, shape and size, brand, chemical composition, quality, trade mark, packaging, durability etc. For example, firms produce different kinds of bathing soap e.g. Hamam, Lux, Lifebuoy, Rexona, Liril, Dove, Ganga, Pears, Le Sancy etc. but these products are close substitutes.

(3) Freedom of entry and exit: Under monopolistic competition the firms are relatively free to enter the industry and to exit from the industry, but they have no absolute freedom of entry the industry. New firms are free to enter into the market with new brands as close substitute of the existing brands.

(4)	Non-price competition: Under monopolistic competition firms compete with one another without changing the price of their products. The firms attract the potential buyers by offering them gifts, incentives, credit schemes, selling schemes and other services. Thus, the firms compete at other than price front.

(5)	Price policy: Every firm has its own price policy. As under monopoly and monopolistic competition the average revenue curve and marginal revenue curve are sloping downward means that the firm will have to fix low price for fulfilling sales maximisation as shown in diagram 7.2 and high price for less sales.

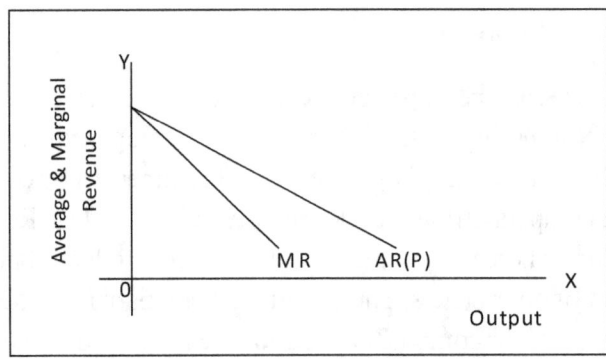

Diagram 7.2

(6)	Less Mobility: There is no perfect mobility of factors of production and of goods and services in practical life. The factors are less mobile because of psychological reasons and disparity among the regions.

(7)	No perfect knowledge: Under monopolistic competition the buyers and sellers do not have perfect knowledge about the market conditions. The buyers and sellers of the products and owners of the factors of production are ignorant about the prices of the products and factor services.

(8)	Selling Costs: Under monopolistic competition each firm wants to promote the sales of its products by incurring selling costs. The expenditure incurred on advertisement and publicity to increase sales is called selling costs. The selling costs shift the demand for a firm's product and the rival firms also retaliate by incurring more and more selling costs.

(9)	Close Substitutes: Under monopolistic competitions the product are not homogeneous products but they are close substitutes to each other which tends to create competition among the firms regarding their products.

(10)	Group Equilibrium: Under monopolistic competition the industry is not said to be in equilibrium but there is a position of group equilibrium for the group as whole e.g. soap manufacturing group combine a group of soap manufacturers and that group itself needs to be in equilibrium position. Group denotes the collection of firms producing unidentical but close substitutes.

## (2)	OLIGOPOLY:

An oligopoly is a market structure in which there are a few sellers of a product selling identical or differentiated products. If they are selling identical products, it is a case of pure oligopoly and if they are selling differentiated products, it is a case of differentiated oligopoly. In this case each firm has to take into account the price being charged by the others. One studies the reaction curves of the other firms and in this way the firms are interdependent. They may even charge high price if they enter into agreement and there is no pricing policy under oligopoly because of the kinky shape of demand curve which is a broken one. Thus, price rigidity and price war are the common features of oligopoly.

The various features of oligopoly are discussed as follows:

(1) Relatively small number of sellers: There are relatively small number of sellers under oligopoly market structure selling identical or differentiated products. Each seller controls a large part of the demand and the policies of every seller influence the price and output of the industry as a whole.

(2) Interdependence of the firms: Under the oligopoly market structure all the firms are sailing in the same boat and every tilting position influences each of the firm as well with equal proportion. No firm can be neutral. They depend on each other while determining the price and output of the firm.

(3) Price rigidity and price war: Price rigidity and price was are the common features of an oligopoly market structure. Each firm retaliates and acts according to the actions of the other firms and a tug of war starts between them which is better known as 'Price War' which further paves way to price rigidity.

(4) Difficulty in entry and exit: Under oligopoly the entry and exit of the firms is banned. The new firms cannot enter the market as the old firms have complete hold over the market conditions and the firms are also reluctant to leave because of the huge investment made by them.

(5) Selling costs: Under oligopoly market structure, each firm pursues an aggressive and defensive marketing strategy to control the market. Advertisement is an important method used by the oligopolists to control the bigger part of the market.

(6) Indeterminateness of the demand curve: Under oligopoly market structure the shape of the demand curve is broken and is indeterminate because the firms cannot assume that the rival firms will not make a change in their price policy in response to change in price affected by it. Thus, the fact that the reaction pattern of the rival firms are indeterminate leaves the demand curve in a indeterminate position.

(7) Complex Market Structure: The market structure of oligopoly is quite complex. As there is a possibility of rival firms to end rivalry by working out some policy of collusion and the collusive oligopoly manifests itself in the form of combination of rival firms to fix the same price and also share in output as in case of cartels. Besides it, non-collusive oligopoly is also found in practice which presents a complex market structure.

(3) DUOPOLY:

When there are only two firms in a market having complete hold over the supply of the product it is termed as a case of duopoly. It is such a market structure when two firms produce a standardised product or produce two products which are very much similar to each other and price of both the products is also uniform. Under such market, each firm has to think over the possible impact on the rival firm of its price policy, discount policy and production techniques. Both the firms try to maximize the profits of each other and by pacts and collusion they try to come in monopoly power situation and exploit the consumers.

DIFFERENT MARKET STRUCTURES AT A GLANCE:

Points of Difference	Perfect Competition	Monopoly	Imperfect Competition		
			Monopolistic competition	Oligopoly	Duopoly
No. of sellers	Very large	One	Large	A few	Two
Product	Homogeneous	One Product	Product differentiation	Product differentiation	Similar of product differentiation
Price	Uniform	Single Price and Price discrimination	Different	Different	Similar or Different
Entry	Free entry	Restricted	Not absolute freedom	Not absolute freedom	Not restricted and absolute freedom
Mobility	Perfect	Partial	Partial	Partial	Partial
Price elasticity of demand	Perfectly elastic	Highly inelastic	Less elastic	Less elastic	Less elastic or inelastic
Knowledge of the market	Perfect knowledge	Partial knowledge	Partial knowledge	Partial knowledge	Partial knowledge
Selling cost	NIL	NIL	Exist	Exist	May or may not exist
AR & MR	Horizontal and AR = MR	Both are different AR > MR	Both are different AR > MR	AR is indeterminate	Downward sloping AR>MR
Transportation cost	NIL	Exist	Exist	Exist	Exist
Price determination	By industry equilibrium	By firm but firm and industry is same	Firms them-selves	Counter pricing	Uniformity

7.5 Summary

Perfect competition is a utopian market situation or a myth. Monopoly is an extreme market situation and consumer has to pay exorbitant prices in it. In case of imperfect competition a lot of selling cost in incurred and the poor consumer bears all the burden of non-price competition or selling cost. Then which market situation is good from the consumer's point of view? What is good for the consumer may be imaginary market situation. Hence, what is prevailing is good. Imperfect competition seems to be much near to the reality in the market. Perfect competition and monopoly both are two extremes. Monopoly is not advantageous to buyer and perfect competition is not that much advantageous to seller. Hence, imperfect competition seems to be an in-between solution.

7.6 Key Words

- **Market:** A place where buyers & sellers are actively engaged in buying and selling acts.

- **Market Structure:** Market structure is called characteristics of market.

- **Perfect Competition:** It is characterized by the presence of many firms and they all sell identical product, the seller is a price taker not price maker.

- **Monopoly:** Market structure, which there is only a single seller of the product.

- **Imperfect Market:** Here many seller of the product but the product of each seller is different from other seller.

- **Monopolistic Competition:**   It is the mid-way between perfect competition & monopoly.

- **Oligopoly:** In this market structure, there are a few sellers of a product selling identical or differentiated products.

- **Duopoly:** Only two firms in a market having complete hold over the supply of the product.

7.6 Self Assesment Test

1.   Define Market.

2.   What are the essentials of a market?

3.   Give the characteristics of Perfect Competition.

4.   What is Monopoly and what are its characteristics?

5.   What is imperfect competition and its forms?

6.   What are the characteristics of Monopolistic competition?

7.   What is oligopoly and what are its characteristics?

8.   Compare Oligopoly and Monopoly.

7.8 Suggested Books/References

1.   Gupta, E.S. : Managerial Economics, Tata MC Grow Hill, New Delhi

2.   Dholakiya R.H. and A.H. Ojha: Micro Economics for Management students, Oxford University Press, Delhi.

8 Pricing Under Different Market Conditions

Unit Structure

8.0   Objectives

After studying this unit, you should be able to understand:-

- The concept of market
- The objective of price output decision
- Price output under Perfect Competition
- Price and output under Monopoly
- Price and output under monopolistic condition
- Pricing and output under Oligopoly

8.1   Introduction

Market:- In general, market means a place where there are many buyers and sellers of different products who are actively engaged in buying and selling acts. The firm's demand curve is expected to depend on such things as the number of sellers in the market and the similarity of their products. These are the aspects of market structure which may be termed as the characteristics of market of generalisation that are likely to influence firm's behaviour and performance. In broader sense face to face contact between buyers and sellers is not necessary. They can establish contact through different means of communication like letters, agents, telegraphs, telephone etc. or newspapers. Thus, the term market does not mean any particular place but the entire area where buyers and sellers of a commodity are in such close contact with each other that the price of the same commodity tends to be one throughout that area.

The market environment is a marketing term and refers to all of the forces outside marketing that affect marketing management's ability to build and maintain successful relationships with target customers. The market environment consists of both the macroenvironment and the microenvironment.

The microenvironment refers to the forces that are close to the company and affect its ability to serve its customers. It includes the company itself, its suppliers, marketing intermediaries, customer markets, competitors, and public.

The company aspect of microenvironment refers to the internal environment of the company. This includes all departments, such as management, finance, research and development, purchasing, operations

84

and accounting. Each of these departments has an impact on marketing decisions. For example, research and development have input as to the features a product can perform and accounting approves the financial side of marketing plans and budgets.

The suppliers of a company are also an important aspect of the microenvironment because even the slightest delay in receiving supplies can result in customer dissatisfaction. Marketing managers must watch supply availability and other trends dealing with suppliers to ensure that the product will be delivered to customers in the time frame required in order to maintain a strong customer relationship.

8.2 Objective of Price Output Decision

- In decision-making analysis, market structure and pricing has an important role through its impact on the decision-making environment.

- Pricing and market structure is important because it affects market outcomes through its impact on the motivations, opportunities and decisions of economic actors participating in the market.

- The goal of economic market structure and pricing analysis is to isolate these effects in an attempt to explain and predict market outcomes.

- There is close relationship between the price and demand of product.

- Pricing must take into account the competitive and legal environment in which the company operates.

8.3 Price Output Decisions Under Perfect Competition

Perfect competition is a market situation where there are large number of buyers and sellers of a homogeneous product and the price of the product is determined by the market forces in an industry. Only single price prevails in the market and all the time products are sold at the prevailing price.

PRICE AND OUTPUT DETERMINATION UNDER SHORT PERIOD:

A firm is said to be in equilibrium in short period where marginal cost (MC) is equal to marginal revenue (MR) and the curve MC cuts MR from below. This also determines the level of output. A short period is the period in which all factors of production cannot be changed, only variable factors like labour, raw material etc. can be changed for the change in the level of output. Hence, short period is such a period in which no firm enters or leaves an industry.

Under equilibrium position, a firm in short period can have the following situations:

(1) Super Normal profit or Profit situation.
(2) Normal profit situation.
(3) Loss situation.
(4) A case of shut down point.

(1) **Super normal profit or a profit situation:** As depicted in the diagram 8.1 average revenue (AR) is equal to marginal revenue (MR) which is shown by horizontal line parallel to the x-axis and short run average cost (SAC) and short run marginal cost (SMC) have also been shown in the diagram.

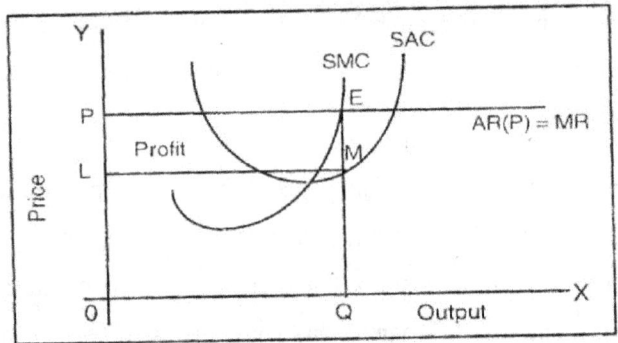

Diagram 8.1

According to the condition of equilibrium of a firm the equilibrium will be at E where SMC equals MR from below and also cuts SAC at its minimum. Hence the price and output are determined at point E. The price is OP and the level of output is OQ.

Average cost = OL or MQ

Then profit per unit = EQ-MQ = EM or PL

Hence,

Total profit of the firm = $\dfrac{\text{Price per unit}}{\text{shaded area}}$ X Total output = PLEM

(2) **Normal profit situation:** Next possible situation in short period can be of a normal profit. When there is no profit i.e. average cost equals the average revenue or price per unit. In diagram 7.2 OP is the price given by the industry and SMC also cuts MR from below and at its point E, SMC and SAC, AR and MR are all equal. Hence, the level of output is determined equal to OQ and the price charged by the firm is OP or EQ.

Average Cost = EQ

Profit per unit = EQ-EQ = Zero

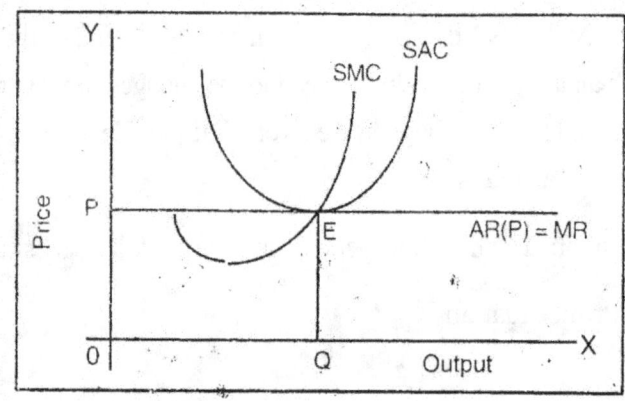

Diagram 8.2

Hence, at this point of equilibrium E the firm is has normal profit i.e. no profit i.e. no profit situation. Normal profit situation is a situation in which a firm neither makes a profit nor makes a loss. Normal profit is a minimum revenue a firm must get to continue in the industry. Normal profit situation not only covers

86

explicit cost but also covers the implicit cost of production i.e. cost of owners own resources engaged in production.

(3) **Loss situation:** Third possibility in short period under perfect competition may be of a loss situation where the prevailing market price may be less than the average cost of the firm that is to say that AR is less than its MC. In such situation the firm will be incurring losses which is well depicted in Diagram 8.3

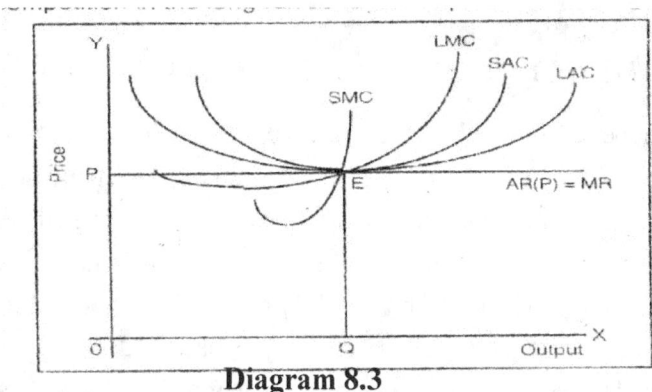

Diagram 8.3

Here in equilibrium at a point E and output is determined equal to OQ and OP is the price charged by the firm. At point E, SMC cuts MR from below and SAC at its minimum.

Per unit price = OP or EQ

Per unit cost = OL or MQ

Per unit Loss = ME (=MQ-EQ)

Hence, total loss = LP ME is shown by the shaded area. Under loss situation all the firms will incur losses and many firms will try to make exit from the industry but due to short period they will be unable to do so. But at the equilibrium position E the firms will be incurring minimum losses.

(4) **A case of shut down point**: The position is very much clear that in a short period situation the firm can neither enter can exit. Now the question arises whether the firms will continue production or break away, the answer is that the firm will continue production up to a particular level if it is able to meet its variable cost of production but if AR is less than its average variable cost (AVC) then it will close its doors and stop production this is well depicted as in diagram 8.4

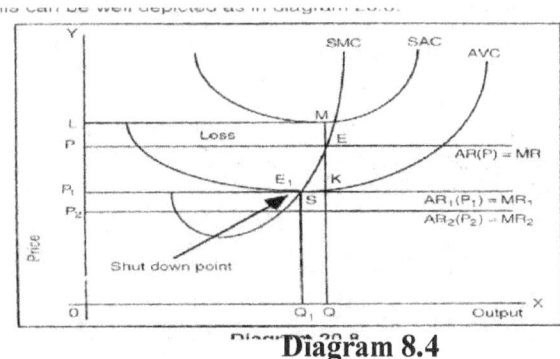

Diagram 8.4

It is also further elaborated that when the price falls so much that the firm is not able to meet even its variable cost then it is advisable to stop the production in the short period. The shut down point arises at that point where the price is below the variable cost. Thus, in short period when the price is less than the variable cost then it will stop production. When the price is OP then the level of output is OQ and firm is

87

incurring losses equal to LP ME at equilibrium point E. When the price is OP then output will be less as before equal to OQ1 and the equilibrium is at E1. Here the firm is meeting its average variable cost and if the price reduces beyond this to OP2 then it will close its doors. Thus, E is the shut down point of the firm where price is equal to average variable cost (P=AVC). At point E1 the firm is not meeting any fixed cost but meeting its variable cost. Here the firm is indifferent, if it stops products on, then it will incur losses equal to fixed cost. Hence, it can be said that the firm is indifferent, it can either stop the production or continue its production. In both the situations the firm is having the same losses. Thus E1 is the shut down point of the firm.

PRICE AND OUTPUT DETERMINATION UNDER THE LONG PERIOD

Long run is that period in which all the factors of production, production as well as technique, size of the plant etc can be adjusted for production according to its demand and any firm can enter or exit. Thus, in the long run every firm is enjoying the normal profit. If in long run the firms make super normal profit then other firms will enter the industry and start production which will increase the supply side and lower down the price. Hence, there will be normal profits. On the other hand if the firms are incurring losses then the firms will exit from the industry and the supply will decrease so as to increase the price, the losses will disappear and the situation of normal profit will prevail under perfect competition in the long run as is well depicted in the diagram 8.5

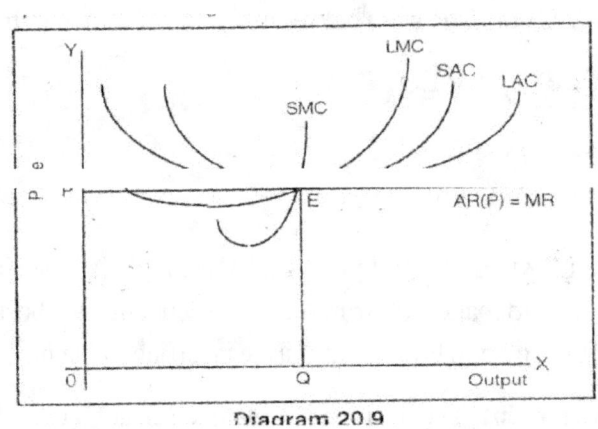

Diagram 20.9

Diagram 8.5

Here is long run the firm will be in equilibrium at E, OP is the price and OQ is the level of output. In long run the equilibrium will be where

MR = MC

AR = AC

or AR = MR = AC = MC

and at point E this condition is fulfilled. The long run equilibrium equation in perfect competition is.

(SAC = SMC = LAC = LMC = AR = MR = P)

Per unit price (AR) = OP or EQ

Average cost (AC) = EQ

Output = OQ

Profit = AR-AC i.e. EQ-EQ = 0.

Here the firm is earning normal profits. Here the price will not be more then OP because of long run. Other firm will enter and on the other hand the same situation will be there. If the price is less than OP then firm will incur losses and the firm will leave the industry because of long run.

88

8.4   Price and Output Decisions Under Monopoly

Monopoly is such a market structure in which there is a single seller of the product. Pure monopoly refers to a firm producing products which have no close substitutes, which is a rare phenomenon. For the monopoly to exist it is necessary to have producer of the product with no close substitutes of the products but there are strong barriers to entry into the industry. In monopoly there is no difference between firm and industry. Firm and industry is the same which always faces a negatively sloped demand curve for its products. Hence, the monopolist is a price maker not a price-taker. Monopoly therefore, refers to that market in which a single firm controls the whole supply of a particular product which has no close substitutes.

PRICE AND OUTPUT DETERMINATION UNDER SHORT PERIOD

Under monopoly market structure a monopolist can make a change in the level of production with making a change in scale of production or with intensive use of the productive technique keeping in view the time factor which enables the monopolist to do this, is called short period. If a monopolist has to produce more he can employ more of labour and can change in quantity of raw material and power resources as required by him. In short period a monopolist cannot influence the fixed costs but variable costs can only be influenced in the matters of taking decision regarding value and production. A monopolist in short period cannot charge price less than the average variable cost (AVC) and if he charges then he will have to close the door of his firm. Thus a monopolist will remain producing until his marginal cost (MC) equals his marginal revenue (MR) and on this point he enjoys maximum profits. Under short period a monopolist may have super normal profit, normal profits or the losses which is discussed as under.

A case of super-normal profit under short period: Diagram 8.6 shows the short period equilibrium of the firm where the monopolist has maximum of the profits. In diagram AR and MR are the Average Revenue and Marginal Revenue curves of the firm and AC and MC are in Average cost and Marginal cost curves of the firm. The firm's MC curve cuts MR curves at point E and establishes equilibrium at point E. At this point the firm's output is OQ and the price is equal to OP and OR or QM is the average cost of the firm. The difference of OP and OR shows profit equal to PR (per unit profit). Thus, PR MT the shaded area represents the supernormal profit of a monopolist under short period.

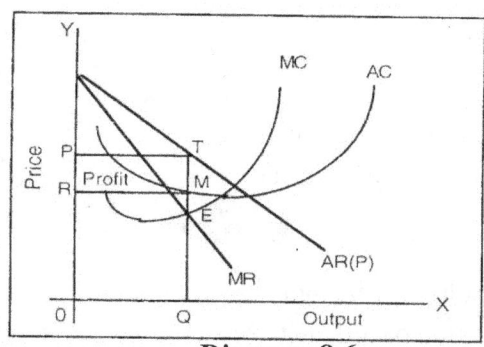

Diagram 8.6

A case of normal profit under short period: Under monopoly market a firm may have normal profit situation which is well illustrated in the diagram 8.7

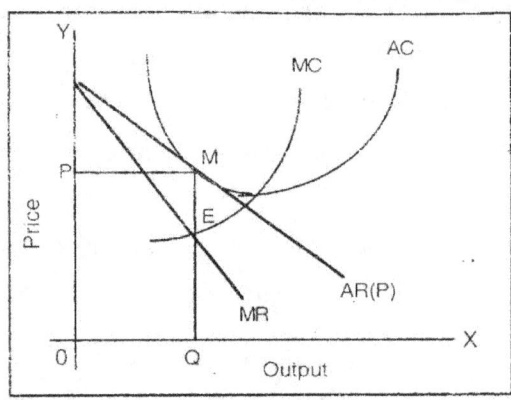

Diagram 21.2

In this diagram, AR and MR are the Average Revenue and Marginal Revenue curves of the firm and AC and MC are the Average cost and Marginal cost curve in the short period. Marginal cost curve cuts marginal revenue curve at point E and also establishes equilibrium at E point and the output level is OQ with OP level of price and QM is the average cost of the firm which is equal to its price (OP). At this position the firm is neither having profits nor incurring losses.

A case of losses under short period: Under monopoly market structure a firm may incur losses which can be depicted in diagram 8.8

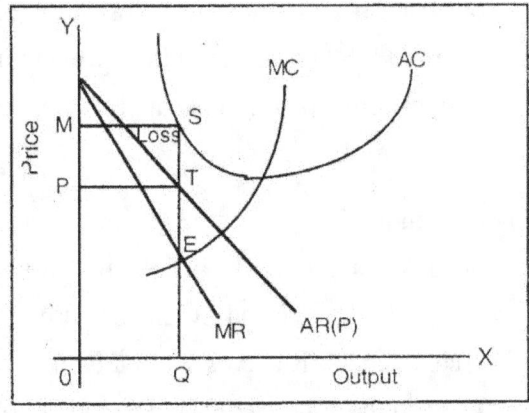

Diagram 8.8

The diagram illustrates a position of losses in short period by a monopolist. Here, price is less than its cost. In diagram SMC and SAC are the short run marginal cost curve and short run average cost curve of the firm respectively. AR and MR are the average revenue and marginal revenue curves of the firm.

SMC cuts the MR at point E and establishes the equilibrium. Here OQ is the level of output to be produced. OP is the price and QM is the average cost of the produce in short period which results in loss equal to OM-OP = PM per unit of output making a total loss equal to the shaded area PMST.

PRICE AND OUTPUT DETERMINATION UNDER LONG PERIOD -

Under long period a monopolist has enough time to adjust the supply according to the demand of the product. In the long period a monopolist will remain in business only if he can make a profit by producing the optimum level of output with the most appropriate scale of plant. The optimum level of output in the long period is given by the point where the LMC curve intersects the MR curve from below and the most appropriate scale of plant is that whose SAC curve is tangent to the LAC curve at the best level of output and the firm or the industry will be in equilibrium. As new entry into the industry in restricted and the firm is the industry as well, the monopolist will adjust the long run output by means of size of plant adjustment depending upon the level and slope of the AR and MR curves.

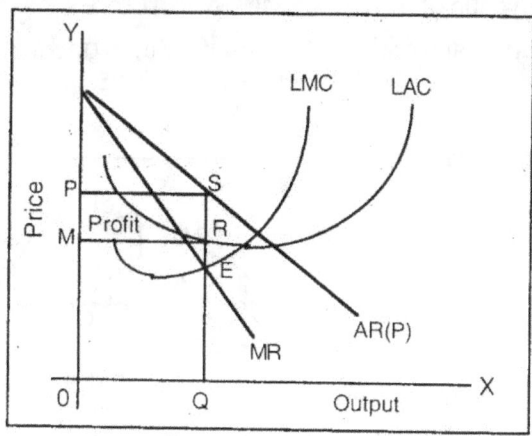

Diagram 8.9

In the long run the firm will be in equilibrium where firm's LMC curve cuts the long run MR curve and at this point of intersection the firm will enjoy profits. Generally, the firm in the long period is earning super-normal profit as shown by diagram 8.9

In the diagram the firm at point E is in equilibrium where LMC cuts MR from below. Thus, E is the equilibrium point where OQ is the output and OP is the price and OM is the average cost of the firm (OM = PQ), hence, the firm is having profit equal to shaded area MPSR. This is a case of profit in long run situation.

8.5 Price and Output Decisions Under Monopolistic Condition

Monopolistic competition is a situation of imperfect competition. In the previous chapters we have discussed the perfect competition and monopoly. Both the situations are exceptions to the market structure and the former is imaginary and not found in the real world.

PRICE AND OUTPUT DETERMINATION OF A FRIM UNDER MONOPOLISTIC COMPETITION : A CASE OF SHORT PRIOD EQUILIBRIUM:

The analysis of short period equilibrium of a firm under monopolistic competition is based on the following assumptions:

(1) Large number of sellers who behave independently.

(2) Product of each seller is different (i.e. product differentiation).

(3) The firm has determinate demand curve (AR) which is elastic.

(4) No new firms enter the industry in short period situation.

(5) Short run cost curves of each firms differ from the other.

(6) Factor services are in perfectly elastic supply.

Given these assumptions, each firm fixes such price and output as maximizes its profit. The equilibrium price and output is determined at a point where the short period marginal cost equals marginal revenue. Since the cost differs in short period, a firm can earn normal profits, super normal profit or incur losses. This analysis can be very well depicted in the following diagram 8.10

The diagram 8.10 (a) 8.10 (b) and 8.10 (c) shows the super normal profit situation, normal profit situation and losses situation of a firm under monopolistic competition in the short period. AR and MR are average revenue and marginal revenue of the firms SMC and SAC are short period marginal cost curves and short period average cost curves and of the corresponding firms operating under monopolistic competition in short period.

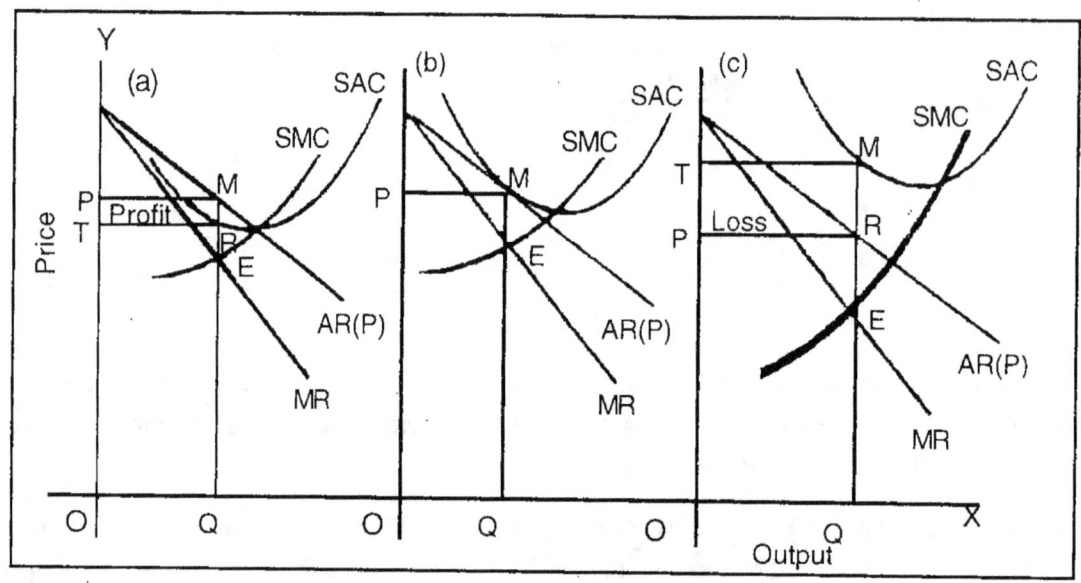

Diagram 8.10

In diagram 8.10 (a) the short period marginal cost curves (SMC) intersects the marginal revenue curve (MR) at point E from below which establishes equilibrium at E point. Here the total output is produce equal to OQ, and the price (per unit) OP is maintained and the cost per unit is OT or RQ. Hence the difference between price and cost i.e. (OP-OT=PT) shows the profits of the firm, then the total profit at equilibrium position (E) would be

PT × OQ (OQ = TR) = PTMR

Thus, the firm enjoys super normal profit equal to the area PTMR in short period under monopolistic competitive market structure.

Likewise, the diagram 8.10 (b) shows the normal profit situation of a firm under short period in a monopolistic competitive market. The diagram depicts the same equilibrium point E which is derived with intersection of SMC and MR and E point shows the same price and same cost for the product i.e. OP is the per unit price of the product and MQ or OP (as MQ = OP) is the cost (per unit) of the product. Here both price and cost are equal and same and the difference which determines the size of the profits is nil. Thus, here the firms enjoy normal profit. It just covers its short-run average unit cost as represented by the tangency of demand curve (AR) and the short period average cost curve (SAC) at M earns normal profits.

The diagram 8.10 (c) shows a situation where the firms is unable to cover its short period average cost (SAC) and tends to incur losses. The equilibrium point E is established as SMC equals MR but the short period average cost is higher than its average revenue and the firm has to incur losses. In this situation. MQ or OT is the cost per unit which is higher than the price (AR) where price per unit is equal to OP and their difference shows the losses (i.e. OT - OP = PT loss per unit) and total output produced is equal to OQ then the total loss then firm would incur is equal to the area PTMR. This area PTMR shows the losses of the firm and the firm in short period will continue its production in the hope of lowering down its costs in the long period under monopolistic market structure.

Hence, it should be remembered that in the short period under monopolistic competition the individual firm may be in equilibrium position but the group as a whole is not in stable equilibrium because the number of firms will have a tendency to change. The existence of full equilibrium, for the group is now here to be seen in the short period under monopolistic competitive market structure.

PRICE AND OUTPUT DETERMINATION UNDER MONOPOLISTIC COMPETITION: A CASE OF LONG PERIOD EQUILIBRIUM:

In the long period the price and output policy of an individual firm is determined by the one general principle where Marginal revenue (MR) and Marginal cost (MC) are equal to each other as shown in the short period. The firm can maximise its net profits by equating the long run marginal cost with its marginal revenue. In long period the individual firm as well as the group as a whole remain in stable equilibrium whereas in short period the individual firm is in equilibrium but the group is not in stable equilibrium. So, it is possible to achieve the full equilibrium position in the long period under monopolistic competitive market structure. To achieve the position of full equilibrium in the long run two adjustments have to be made.

(1) All the quantity offered for sale must be equal to its demand in the market at a given price.

(2) Entry and exit of firms in response to the general position of the existing firm.

The first type of adjustment is similar to that of perfect competition. But under monopolistic competition all the firms do not charge the same price. They charge different prices but the differentials are too much. So, under monopolistic competition there is a general level of price and also a general level of AR (Average Revenue) curves of the individual firms. Each firm adjusts its price and output in such a way that LMC must equal to MR and therefore, each firm determines its output independently. The summation of the output of the firms provide us the total output available for sale in the market as shown by diagram 8.11. It is assumed here that entry of new firm is restricted.

In diagram 8.11 AR and MR are the average revenue and marginal revenue curve of the firm. LMC and LAC are the long period marginal cost curve and long period average cost curve of the firm. Every firm equates its marginal cost to its marginal revenue. In the diagram E1 is the point of equilibrium when the entry of new firms is restricted then the firms enjoying super-normal profits with the OQ level of output as OP is the price and EQ or OM is cost per unit of product and difference between the two shows the profit situation (i.e. OP-OM = MP) profit per unit and total output is OQ hence, total profit is MP × OQ) equal to the area MPTE. Thus, MPTE is the super-normal profit of a firm under long period situation when the entry of the new firms is restricted but this profit situation will attract other firms to enter.

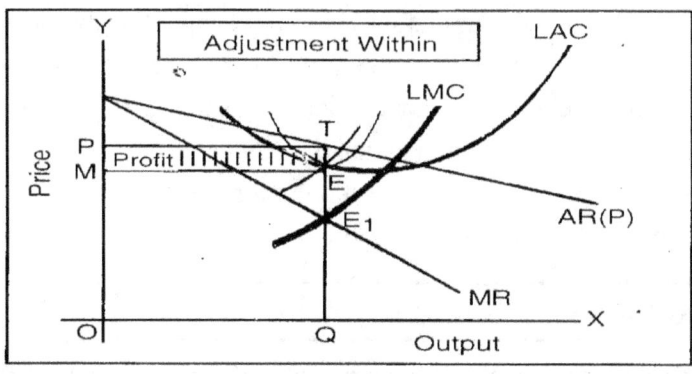

Diagram 8.11

93

WITH OPEN ENTRY:

If the monopolistic competitive industry is earning supernormal profits new firms will be attracted towards the group. With

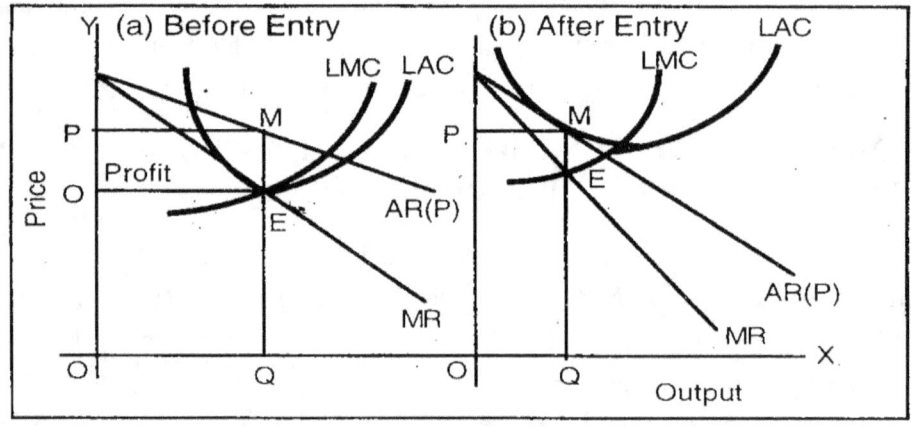

Diagram 8.12

the entry of the new firms in the industry the super-normal profit tends to decline and a situation of normal profit will prevail. With entry of the new firms, the existing market is divided among more sellers so that each firm may sell lesser quantity of goods than before resulting the demand curve to shift downward. And at the entry of new firm, increase in demand will cause the individual cost curve to shift upward. This two way shifting i.e. the demand to downward and cost to upward squeezes the position of super-normal profit. Hence in the long run the firm earns only normal profits which is depicted in the diagram 9.18 as under.

Before the entry of the new firms in the industry under monopolistic competition the firm is in equilibrium at point E where LMC cuts MR and OQ level of output is produced and OP level of price is maintained, EQ or OC is the cost per unit and OP is the price per unit thus PC is the profit per unit with which accrue to firm thus CPME is the super normal profit accrued to the firm in the long run when there is no entry in the industry which is well shown in the diagram 8.11 (a)

Similarly, the diagram 8.11 (b) depicts the normal profits situation when there is free entry. The new firms will be attracted when the existing are earning super-normal profits and with the entry of the new firms the demand curve will slope downward and the price will also lower down and ultimately at the point of equilibrium position at E, OP is price and MQ is the cost per unit of production leaving the firms with normal profit with OQ level of output.

If the firms do not earn super normal profits under monopolistic competition they will not incur losses either because under loss situation the firm will exit from the industry, as to decrease the supply and price to go up and resources will be in surplus and will become cheaper than before to decrease the cost which further will eliminate the losses as shown in diagram 8.11 (b). This long run equilibrium analysis under monopolistic competition reveals that each individual firm and the whole industry do not produce optimum level of output as is clear from the diagram that the point M is tangent point which is not lowest considering the cost conditions, whereas L is the lowest point for the cost conditions and for the firms to produce. Thus, under monopolistic competition in the long run situation there is excess capacity.

8.6 Pricing and Output Decisions Under Oligopoly

The word oligopoly is derived from the Greek words (i.e. Oligos + Pollen); Oligos means few and pollen means to sell. It is also a situation of imperfect competition where there are a few sellers of a particular product or a differentiated product. When the firms are selling homogeneous product then it is a case of 'pure oligopoly' and when the firms are selling differentiated product, then it is case of differentiated oligopoly. According to Stigler, "Oligopoly is that market situation in which a firm bases its market policy in part on the expected behaviour of a few close rivals." To make the meaning more clear oligopoly is that form of imperfect competition where there are few firms in the market, producing either an homogeneous product or producing products which are close but not perfect substitutes of each other.

PRICE AND OUTPUT DETERMINATION UNDER OLIGOPOLY:

Generally the firm is in equilibrium position where its marginal cost curves equals its marginal revenue curves and price is depicted with the help of average revenue curve or demand cure. But this analysis is not true in the case of oligopolistic situation because of the interdependence of the firms and indeterminateness of the demand curve and considerable distinction in the allocation of common cost to specific products, with the result that there is no single definite cost curve. Price and output determination can be studied under the following three situations:

(1) Independent pricing (2) Pricing under collusion and (3) Pricing under Price Leadership.

Independent Pricing: Under oligopolistic market situation each firm tries to follow an independent price and output policy. The price fixed by each firm may be more or less than monopoly price, because each firm produces a differentiated product. And on the basis of fixing the prices in a competitive manner, the price war breaks out between the firms. Thus, there can be two limits; the upper limit laid down by the monopoly price and the lower limit is determined by the actual price which may come to be fixed under oligopolistic conditions. There is no simple theory that explains where the actual price will be set between these limits which further depends on the circumstances and conditions prevailing in the market. In case where the firms are producing similar products and all the firms in existence are showing the market proportionately and equally, then a uniform pricing policy is to be fixed by them. But in case of differentiated products as discussed earlier each oligopolistic firm is in such a position as to fix the price like a monopolist.

But some modern economists say that free price policy is not found in the real situation because of the wrong assumptions like identical products, iso-cost, equal and proportionate distribution of market etc. So, under oligopoly the price does not remain stable. The economists are of the view that behaviour of an oligopolistic market is indeterminate. What they mean is that its behaviour cannot be explained by the same conceptual apparatus that applies to other market structures. The independent pricing under oligopolistic market leads to lot of uncertainty, insecurity and antagonism in the market. It is because of this uncertainty, insecurity and antagonism some economists points out that independent price setting under oligopoly cannot remain for a longer period and it will further be replaced by other forms of price fixation. Thus, on the basis of uncertainty, insecurity and antagonism independent pricing is not possible under oligopolistic market structure which leads to price war and price rigidity.

Price War : Price war sets in when a firm reduces the price of its product in order to increase its sales and maximise revenue. Its rival firms also resort to cutting down the price of its product so each firm tries to undercut the other which paves way to price war as can be well depicted in the diagram 8.13

'ell depicted in the diagram 24.1.

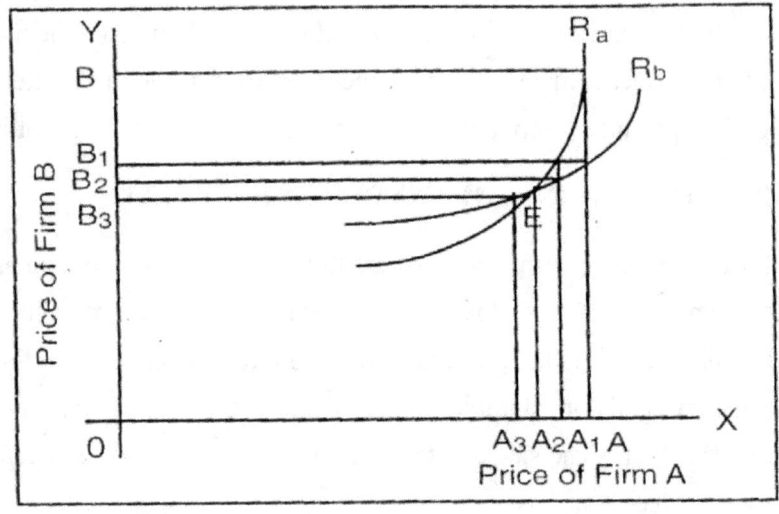

Diagram 8.13

To explain the price war we take two firm A & B with their respective reaction curve Ra and Rb as the price line. The firm A & B whose price moves are taken along X-axis and Y-axis respectively as shown in diagram 8.13 with Ra and Rb respective reactive reaction curves. The curve R focuses the price reaction of firm A and Rb is the reaction curve of firm B. The curve Ra focuses the price reaction of firm A to the price move of firm B, similarly, Rb shows the price reaction of B to the price move of A. Suppose, initially the firm A changes price equal to OA then firm B reacts and cuts its price to OB1 from OB; Further A reacts and charges a price equal to QA1 and B will react to this decline in A's price and B charges a price equal to OB2. This price reduction turns into price war and will continue until both reach at point E where A - firm charges price equal to OA3 and B charges price equal to OB3 and further price cutting will be disastrous for both firm. A and firm B. Thus a position of stable equilibrium is not to be found under oligopolistic market due to the presence of uncertainty, insecurity and antagonism.

Price Rigidity:

The Kinked Demand Curve is also known as Paul M. Sweezy Model. The oligopolistic price that remain stable over a period of time is known as price rigidity. It is such a situation when there is a change in cost of production and demand conditions there is no change in the price of the goods and services from the firm's side. As the price of the durable goods do not change throughout the year say fan, radio, television, watch etc.

Reasons for Price Rigidity:

There are the following reasons which are responsible for price rigidity under oligopolistic market.
(1) When the Oligopolists might happen to understand the basic element that it is futile to exercise price war as price war does favour none.
(2) The oligopolists may be self content with the current prices so as to avoid uncertainty, insecurity, antagonism etc.
(3) The oligopolists may stick to prevailing price so as to discourage the entry of the new firms.
(4) If any price is fixed through collusion or an agreement, no firm is going to change it so as to avoid the fear of price war.

(5) As high selling cost is involved no firm is ready to change its price.

(6) The firm may increase their profits by sales maximisation rather than cutting down the prices. So, price rigidity is maintained.

(7) Finally, the shape of the Kinked Demand Curve goes in support for price rigidity in oligopolistic market structure.

Assumptions of kinked demand curve:

The Kinked demand curve analysis is based on the following assumption:

(1) Under oligopolic market an established price prevails.

(2) The behaviour of each firm or seller depends upon its rival.

(3) If one firm raises or reduces the price the same is followed by its rivals.

(4) The marginal cost curve passes through the dotted portion of the Marginal revenue curve which further explains that changes in marginal cost do not affect price and output under oligopolistic market.

(5) The firms follow non-competitive price policy.

The analysis of price rigidity can be explained with the help of Kinked Demand Curve as under with the help of dia<del>analysis of price rigidity can be explained with the help of</del> <del>ve as under with the help of diagram 24.2.</del>

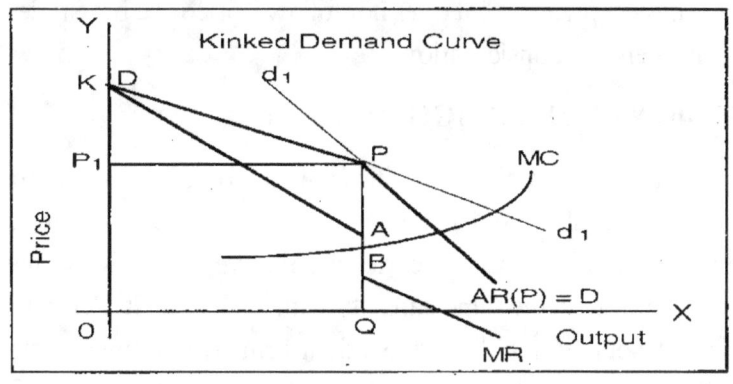

Diagram 24.2

The diagram 8.14 explains that the firm is starting at a point P with the corresponding current price equal to OP1. The diagram shows that KPD is the Kinked demand curve and P is the Kinkey point on the Kinked demand curve KPD, therefore OP1 is the prevailing price in the oligopolistic market with OQ level of output and MR is the discontinuous Marginal Revenue curve, the portion AB shows its discontinuity and MC is the marginal cost curve faced by an oligopolist. Starting from point P with corresponding prevailing prince OP1 any increase in the price will reduce its sales for the firm and rival may or may not follow the same, then the firm will reduce its sales and profit will be limited. It is because of the KP portion of the Kinked demand curve being elastic and the corresponding portion of KA of the Marginal revenue curve is positive. Thus, any increase in price is liable to reduce its sales and revenue frontiers and then profit to decline.

On the contrary, if the firm or seller reduces its price below OP1 its rival firm will also reduce the price of its product which may lead to an increase in its sales but the profit would be less than before. The reason is very clear that PD portion of Kinked demand curve is less elastic and the corresponding part of marginal revenue curve below B is negative. Thus, in both the situations either price increases or price decreases and the oligopolist remains the loser. Thus, the oligopolist would stick to the prevailing market price OP1 which remains rigid. Hence the rigidity is maintained at Kinky point P of the Kinked Demand curve under oligopolistic market. This is such a situation in which the oligopolistic firm does not want to

97

have a change in its price, maintaining rigidity at the Kinky point of the Kinked demand curve. Thus price rigidity is always maintained at the Kinky point on the Kinked demand curve under oligopolistic market. The demand curve KPD with P as Kinky point on it presents a discontinuity in marginal revenue curve equal to the portion AB and beyond B the marginal revenue curve is negative. The elasticity of Kinked demand curve determines the size of discontinuity in the marginal revenue curve. The more elastic the demand curve is to the left of the Kinky point P and more inelastic to right of the Kinky point, the more will be discontinuity in the marginal revenue curve under oligopolistic market in the price rigidity analysis. If the angle, KPD becomes a right angle the gap or discontinuity (AB) will be the widest. Thus, the price will be stable and rigid till marginal cost curve cuts marginal revenue curve, somewhere between the discontinuity portion AB. The Theory of Kinked demand curve has its drawbacks.

(i) The gap or discontinuity or Marginal Revenue Curve (MR) may be unstable.

(ii) The theory does not tell us how the initial price OP1 is maintained.

(iii) Price determination is illusionary as it does not follow the market behaviour.

(iv) It is doubtful about the stability of price under oligopoly as actual sales price in case of many products is not possible.

(v) Kinked theory follows a price cut but does not follow a price rise but Stigler remarked that a price rise has not been taken into consideration.

PERFECT COLLUSION UNDER OLIGOPOLY:

A collusion or a cartel is a combination of firms whose object is to limit the scope of competitive forces within a market. Individual firms of a certain industry surrender to a central association the power to make price and output decisions. Thus, the cartel or collusive oligopoly assumes monopoly power the determines the price and output in the same capacity with zeal and jest. Perfect collusion implies cartel agreements which is an association of the independent firms within the industry. Perfect cartel under oligopoly with complete control over the price and output policy of the member firms and with the threat of entry is a situation for consideration.

(1) Perfect collusion: Perfect cartel is an extreme form of perfect collusion. Each firm reserves profits according to the assigned quota and therefore the principle of cost maximisation is not likely to be followed. Thus, it is also contemplated that price and output results obtained under perfect collusive oligopoly are the same as obtained under monopoly. The price and output under central can be illustrated with the help of following diagram 8.15.

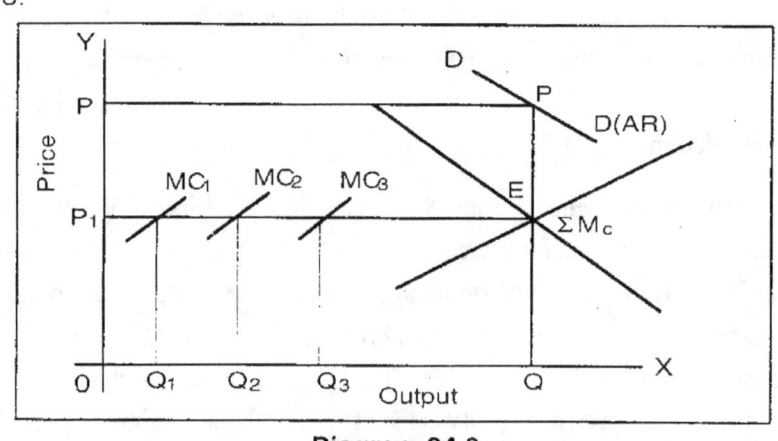

Diagram 24.3

98

In diagram 8.14 DD is the industry demand curve and MR is the corresponding marginal revenue curve taking three oligopolistic firms A, B and C in the industry. Their marginal cost curves are MC1, MC2 and MC3 respectively with OP1 level of price with their respective output equal to OQ1m OQ2 and OQ3. MC is the lateral summation of the marginal cost curves of all the individual firm in the industry which equals Marginal revenue curve at point E with OQ level of output with the price level OP, as DD is the demand curve for the industry and also determines the price for the industry as a whole under the conditions of perfect collusion and each firm will produce that level of output at which marginal cost curves equals industry's marginal revenue curves i.e. EP1. Thus A will produce OQ1, B will produce OQ2 and C will produce OQ3 of the output and OQ being the total output of the industry (OQ1+OQ2+OQ3 = OQ). It results into the maximum joint profit for the industry but it is not necessary that each firm may have profit equal to their quota allotment. Mutual agreement and relative bargaining power determine the division of profit.

(2) Market Sharing Cartel under Oligopoly:

Another form of perfect collusion under oligopolistic market is that of market sharing cartel by the member firms of a cartel. Market sharing cartel is an equal division of total market sales among all its firms. In differentiated oligopoly all firms in an industry enter into a collusion for charging a uniform price which is agreeable to all the firms. They divide the market among themselves according to an agreement and get profits according to its sales and their demand curve will be a part of the demand curve for the industry. As each firm has its own demand curve with the same elasticity as that of industry demand curve which can be illustrated in diagram 8.16

When equal market's sharing DD is the industry demand curve and MR is the corresponding marginal revenue curve (DD1) MC is the aggregate marginal cost curve of the industry. MR curve DD1 intersects MC curve at point E and set OP price and OQ level of output under this situation. Industry output OQ is shared equally by the firms at MC curve of firms cuts MR curve at point C and OQ level of output is determined as OQ level of output is for the industry as a whole. Thus, OQ is just half of the total output QO or OQ0 - QoQ level of output. Thus, equal level of output is shared by the firms. Each firm tries to increase the share of the market by means of secret price concessions which tends to change the demand cost conditions further and price variations among firms become more common and ultimately the agreement becomes a farce and all the firms act independent oligopolists.

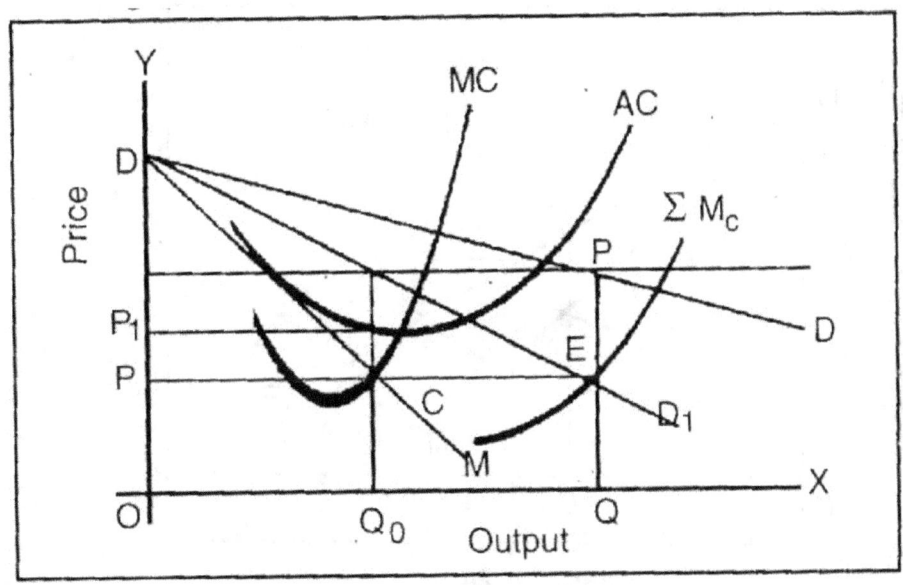

Diagram 8.16

PRICE LEADERSHIP:

Price leadership is imperfect collusion among the oligopolistic firms in an industry with the dominant firm as all firms follow the dominant firm as one of the big firm in an oligopolistic market. There is an agreement among all the firms to sell the product at a price set by the leader of the dominant firm in an industry. Sometimes a meeting is held and a definite agreement is taken by the dominant firm. In case of homogeneous or heterogeneous product the price may be a uniform price and the same is announced by the leader of the firms for example, price leadership industries are like cement, cigarettes, flour, fertilizers, petroleum, milk, steel, etc. Price leadership may be of different types.

(i)   There is a barometric price in which there is no dominant firm which announces the price but the wisest firm announces the price by taking into consideration the demand and cost conditions and the rest follow suit.

(ii) When the price is announced by a dominant firm then it is known as dominant price leadership. It is also known as partial monopolistic price leadership.

(iii) The dominating firm may fix the profit maximisation price for itself and for the others to accept it; it is known as aggressive price leadership. It may fix such a low price as some of the firms may resort to exit from the industry.

(iv) When the pricing is done by the dominant firm suppressing competition among oligopoly firms is known as effective price leadership.

The real test of the dominant firms price leadership is the extent to which the other firms follow its lead. The moment the firms cease to follow the price leader, the model of price leadership by the dominant firm seems to break down. Besides, if the other firms have different cost curves the same price may not maximise short run profits for all the firms under oligopolistic situation under the head of price leadership.

The price leadership firm may keep in mind the following points while exercising price leadership:

1- The reactions of the firms when the price is announced.
2- Elasticity of substitution between the product of the price leadership firm and the competitive firms.
3- Knowledge about the policy of the competitive firms.

The price determination by the price leadership firm can be illustrated with the help of the diagram 8.17

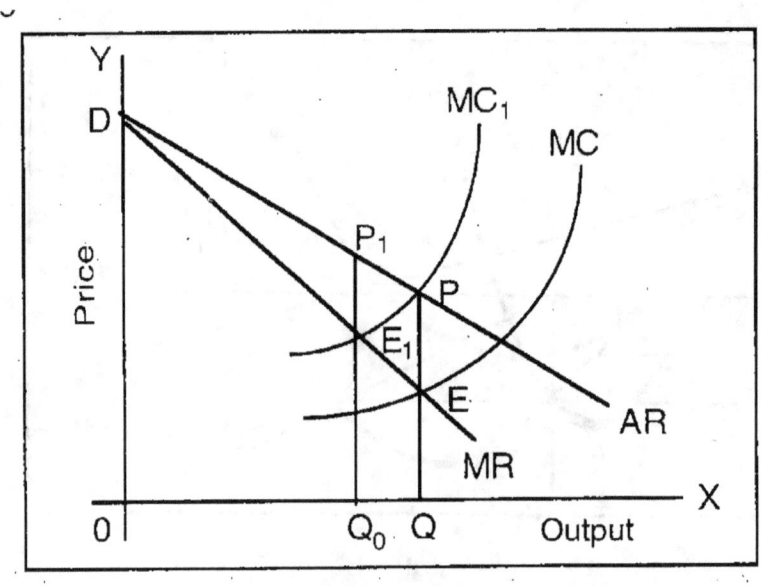

Diagram 24.5

ram. MC and MC₁ are the marginal cost curves of the two firi

100

In this diagram, MC and MC1 are the marginal cost curves of the two firms A & B and AR and MR are their respective average revenue curve and marginal revenue curve. The firm A's marginal cost curve MC and its marginal revenue curve MR intersect each other at E and E is the point of Equilibrium with OQ level of output and QP level of price and similarly, in case of firm B its equilibrium point is also set at point E1 where its respective marginal cost curve MC1 and Marginal revenue curve MR cut each other at point E1 and OQ1 is level of output with OQ1 is level of output with P1Q1, being the price, making a comparison between the two firms firm A's price is lower than the price of firm B but the output is greater than B's firm so, in this way firm A will act as price leadership firm and will determine the price and output policy for the rest of the firms under oligopolistic market under the case of price leadership. Thus, firm A is the price leadership firm which quotes the price for rest of the firms and acts as a torch bearer in the field of pricing and output.

8.7 Summary

Markets are the heart and soul of a capitalist economy, and varying degrees of competition lead to different market structures, with differing implications for the outcomes of the market place. Market structure and pricing decisions are closely related

The degree to which the firm gets to choose price is determined in large part by market structure. These elements are perfect competition, monopolistic competition, oligopoly and monopoly. Based on the differing outcomes of different market structures, economists consider some market structures more desirable, from the point of view of the society, than others. The extent to which an individual firm exercises control over the price of the product it sells is another important characteristic of a market structure. Under perfect competition, an individual firm has no control over the price of the product it sells. A firm under monopolistic competition or oligopoly has some control over the price of the product it sells. Finally, a monopoly firm is deemed to have considerable control over the price of its product.

8.8 Key Words

- **Firm:** One or more than one units which are under the same ownership.

- **Industry:** It is a union of all the individual firms producing the same product.

8.9 Self Assessment Test

1.   Define Market environment.

2.   Explain price output determination under Perfect Competition.

3.   Explain Price and output determination under monopolistic condition with suitable diagram.

4.   Illustrate Pricing and output determination under Oligopoly.

8.10 Suggested Books/Refernces

1.   Mathur N.D., Managerial Economics, Shivam book House (P.) Limited, Jaipur

2.   Mehta P.L. : Managerial Economics-Analysis Problems and Cases: Sultan Chand, New Delhi.

9 Price Discrimination

Unit Structure

9.0   Objectives

After studying this unit, you should be able to understand:

- The concept of price discrimination
- The objectives of price discrimination
- Types of price discrimination
- The concept of dumping
- Price Discrimination-harmful or beneficial to society

9.1   Introduction

Price discrimination or price differentiation exists when sales of identical goods or services are transacted at different prices from the same provider. In a theoretical market with perfect information, perfect substitutes, and no transaction costs or prohibition on secondary exchange (or re-selling) to prevent arbitrage, price discrimination can only be a feature of monopolistic and oligopolistic markets, where market power can be exercised. Otherwise, the moment the seller tries to sell the same goods at different prices, the buyer at the lower price can arbitrage by selling to the consumer buying at the higher price but with a small discount. However, product heterogeneity, market frictions or high fixed costs (which make marginal-cost pricing unsustainable in the long run) can allow for some degree of differential pricing to different consumers, even in fully competitive retail or industrial markets. Price discrimination also occurs when the same price is charged from customers which have different supply costs.

Difference between price discrimination and product differentiation

Product differentiation differentiation of the product gives the supplier greater control over price and the potential to charge consumers a premium price because of actual or perceived differences in the quality / performance of goods or services.

Price discrimination occurs when a firm charges a different price from different groups of consumers for an identical good or service, for reasons not associated with costs.

9.2 Objectives of Price Discrimination

There are several objectives of price discrimination. Some are as given below.

- Firms will be able to increase revenue. This will enable some firms to stay in business which otherwise would have made a loss. For example price discrimination is important for train companies which offer different prices for peak and off peak.

- Increased revenues can be used for research and development which benefit consumers

- Some consumers will benefit from lower fares. Eg. old people benefit from lower train companies, old people are more likely to be poor

- The other objective to the consumer of price discrimination are - price discrimination is likely to increase output and make the good or service available to more people and the increased competition in the market leads to lower prices and more choice.

9.3 Conditions Necessary for Price Discrimination to Work

Essentially there are two main conditions required for discriminatory pricing

1) Differences in price elasticity of demand between markets: There must be a different price elasticity of demand from each group of consumers. The firm is then able to charge a higher price from the group with a more price inelastic demand and a relatively lower price from the group with a more elastic demand. By adopting such a strategy, the firm can increase its total revenue and profits (i.e. achieve a higher level of producer surplus). To profit maximize, profit the firm will seek to set marginal revenue equal to marginal cost in each separate (segmented) market.

2) Barriers to prevent consumers switching from one supplier to another: The firm must be able to prevent "market seepage" or "consumer switching" - defined as a process whereby consumers who have purchased goods or services at a lower price are able to re-sell it to those consumers who would have normally paid the expensive price. This can be done in a number of ways, - and is probably easier to achieve with the provision of a unique service such as a haircut rather than with the exchange of tangible goods. Seepage might be prevented by selling a product to consumers at unique and different points in time - for example with the use of time specific airline tickets that cannot be resold under any circumstances.

The effects of price discrimination on social efficiency are unclear; typically such behavior leads to lower prices for some consumers and higher prices for others. Output can be expanded when price discrimination is very efficient, but output can also decline when discrimination is more effective at extracting surplus from high-valued users than expanding sales to low valued users. Even if output remains constant, price discrimination can reduce efficiency by misallocating output among consumers.

9.4 Types of Price Discrimination

There are many forms of price discrimination, but the standard method of classification identifies three types or degrees of discrimination. But there are other two types also named as skimming and combination. Their common characteristic is that they allow the firm to capture part of the consumer surplus that would have resulted from uniform pricing.

First degree price discrimination

In first degree price discrimination, price varies by customer's willingness or ability to pay. This arises from the fact that the value of goods is subjective. A customer with low price elasticity is less deterred by a higher price than a customer with high price elasticity of demand. As long as the price elasticity (in absolute value) for a customer is less than one, it is very advantageous to increase the price: the seller gets more money for fewer goods. With an increase of the price elasticity tends to rise above one. One can show that in optimum price, as it varies from customer to cuustomer, is inversely proportional to one minus the reciprocal of the price elasticity of that customer at that price. This assumes that the consumer passively reacts to the price set by the seller, and that the seller knows the demand curve of the customer. In practice however there is a bargaining situation, which is more complex: the customer may try to influence the price, such as by pretending to like the product less than he or she really does or by threatening not to buy it.

An alternative way to understand first Degree Price Discrimination is as follows: This type of price discrimination is primarily theoretical because it requires the seller of goods or services to know the absolute maximum price that every consumer is willing to pay. As above, it is true that consumers have different price elasticities, but the seller is not concerned with thus. The seller is concerned with the maximum willingness to pay (or reservation price) of each customer. By knowing the reservation price, the seller is able to absorb the entire market surplus, thus taking all of the consumer's surplus from the consumer and transforming it into revenues. From a social welfare perspective though, first degree price discrimination is not necessarily undesirable. That is, the market is still entirely efficient and there is no deadweight loss to society. In a market with first degree price discrimination, the seller simply captures all surplus. Efficiency is unchanged but the wealth is transferred. This type of market does not exist much in reality, hence it is primarily theoretical. Examples of where this might be observed are in markets where consumers bid for tenders, though still, in this case, the practice of collusive tendering undermines efficiency. It is a classic part of price competition between firms seeking a market advantage or to protect an established market position.

Perfect Price Discrimination - charging whatever the market will bear

Sometimes known as optimal pricing, with perfect price discrimination, the firm separates the whole market into each individual consumer and charges them the price they are willing and are able to pay. If successful, the firm can extract all consumer surplus that lies beneath the demand curve and turn it into extra producer revenue (or producer surplus). This is impossible to achieve unless the firm knows every consumer's preferences and, as a result, is unlikely to occur in the real world. The transactions costs involved in finding out through market research what each buyer is prepared to pay is the main block or barrier to a businesses engaged in this form of price discrimination.

If the monopolist is able to perfectly segment the market, then the average revenue curve effectively becomes the marginal revenue curve for the firm. The monopolist will continue to see extra units as long as the extra revenue exceeds the marginal cost of production.

The reality is that, although optimal pricing can and does take place in the real world, most suppliers and consumers prefer to work with price lists and price menus from which trade can take place rather than having to negotiate a price for each unit of a product bought and sold.

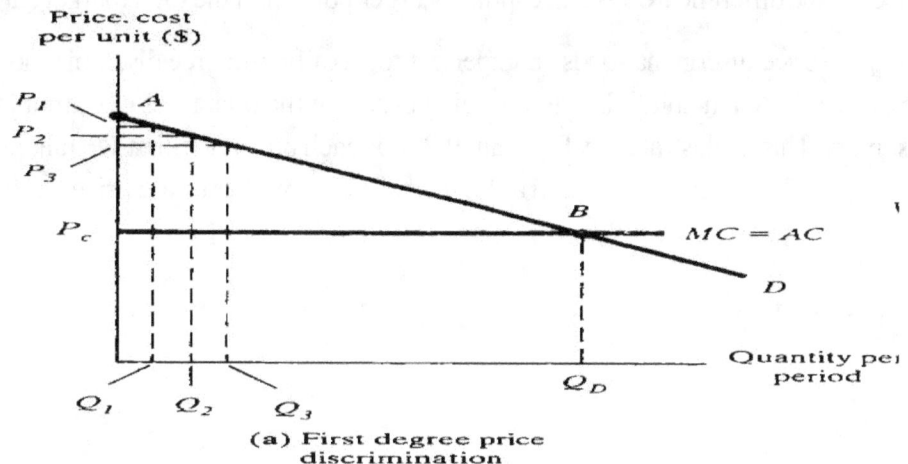

Diagram 9.1

Diagram 9.1 shows the demand curve faced by a monopolist. The curve indicates the maximum price that can be obtained for successive units of output. For example, the first unit Q1, could command a maximum price of P1, the second could be sold for a maximum of P2, and so on. To simplify the discussion, it is assumed that marginal cost is constant and equal to average cost.

First-degree discrimination involves charging the maximum price possible for each unit of output. Thus, the consumer who attaches the greatest value to the product is identified and charged a price of P1. Similarly, the consumers willing to pay P2 for the second unit and P3 for the third are identified and required to pay P2 and P3, respectively.

With first-degree price discrimination, the profit-maximizing output rate is where the marginal cost and demand curves intersect. In Figure 9.1, it occurs at QD. At this point, the maximum price that can be obtained for the product is just equal to the marginal cost of production. Any attempt to sell more than QD units would reduce profits because price would have to be less than marginal cost. Conversely, any rate of output less than QD would not maximize profits because the additional units could be sold (as shown by the demand curve) at prices greater than the marginal cost.

First-degree discrimination is the most extreme form of price discrimination and the most profitable pricing scheme for the firm. Because buyers are charged the maximum price for each unit of output, no consumer surplus remains. Consumer surplus is the difference between the price a consumer is willing to pay and the actual price charged for the good or service. The maximum consumer surplus results when there is no price discrimination, and price is set equal to marginal cost. In Fig 9.1, this maximum consumer surplus is shown as the area of the triangle APcB. In contrast with first-degree price discrimination, there is no consumer surplus because APcB is captured by the firm as economic profit.

Second degree price discrimination

In second degree price discrimination, price varies according to quantity sold. Larger quantities are available at a lower unit price. This is particularly widespread in sales to industrial customers, where bulk buyers enjoy higher discounts.

Additionally to second degree price discrimination, sellers are not able to differentiate between different types of consumers. Thus, the suppliers will provide incentives for the consumers to differentiate themselves according to preference. As above, quantity "discounts", or non-linear pricing, is a means by which suppliers use consumer preference to distinguish classes of consumers. This allows the supplier to set different prices to the different groups and capture a larger portion of the total market surplus.

Second degree price discrimination is an imperfect form of first-degree discrimination. Instead of setting different prices for each unit, it involves pricing based on the quantities of output purchases by individual consumers. This is illustrated by Diagram 9.2. For each buyer, the first Q1 unit purchased are priced at P1, the next Q2 - Q1 units are priced at P2, and all additional units are priced at P3

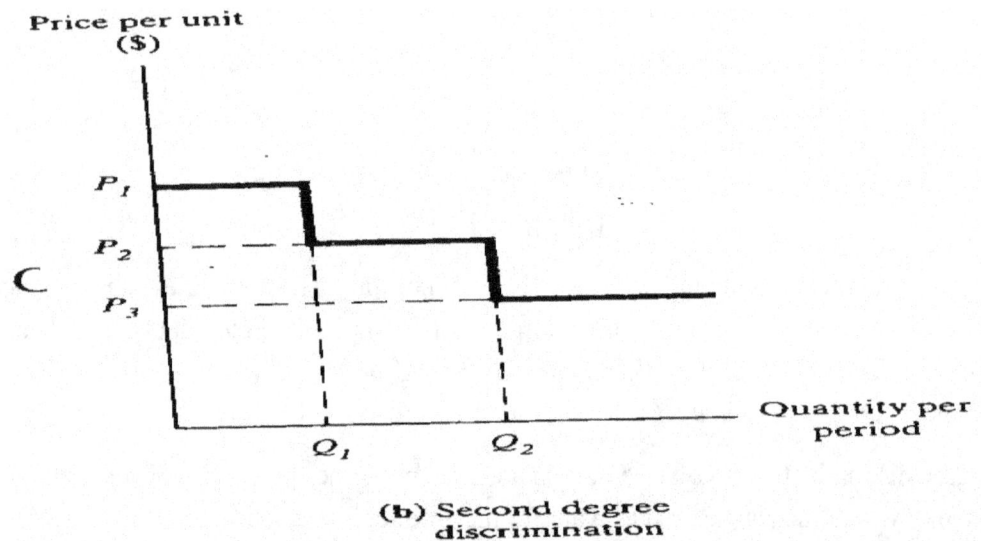

(b) Second degree discrimination

In reality, different pricing may apply to differences in product quality as well as quantity. For example, airlines often offer multiple classes of seats on flights, such as first class and economy class. This is a way to differentiate consumers based on preference, and therefore allows the airline to capture more consumer's surplus.

This type of price discrimination involves businesses selling off packages of a product deemed to be surplus capacity at lower prices than the previously published/advertised price.

Examples of this can often be found in the hotel and airline industries where spare rooms and seats are sold on a last minute standby basis. In these types of industry, the fixed costs of production are high. At the same time the marginal or variable costs are small and predictable. If there are unsold airline tickets or hotel rooms, it is often in the businesses best interest to offload any spare capacity at a discount prices, always providing that the cheaper price that adds to revenue at least covers the marginal cost of each unit.

There is nearly always some supplementary profit to be made from this strategy. And, it can also be an effective way of securing additional market share within an oligopoly as the main suppliers' battle for market dominance. Firms may be quite happy to accept a smaller profit margin if it means that they manage to steal an advantage on their rival firms. The expansion of e-commerce by both well established businesses and new entrants to online retailing has seen a further growth in second degree price discrimination.

Peak and Off-Peak Pricing

Peak and off-peak pricing are common in the telecommunications industry, leisure retailing and in the travel sector. Telephone and electricity companies separate markets by time: There are three rates for telephone calls: a daytime peak rate, and an off peak evening rate and a cheaper weekend rate. Electricity suppliers also offer cheaper off-peak electricity during the night.

106

At off-peak times, there is plenty of spare capacity and marginal costs of production are low (the supply curve is elastic) whereas at peak times when demand is high, we expect that short run supply becomes relatively inelastic as the supplier reaches capacity constraints. A combination of higher demand and rising costs forces up the profit maximising price.

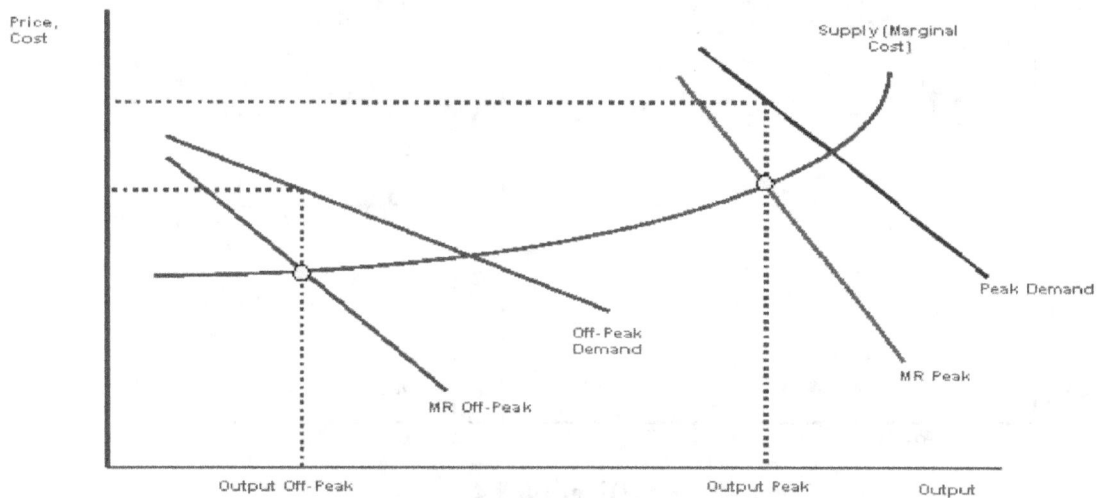

Diagram 9.3

Third degree price discrimination

In third degree price discrimination, price varies by attributes such as location or by customer segment, or in the most extreme case, by the individual customer's identity; where the attribute in question is used as a proxy for ability/willingness to pay.

Additionally to third degree price discrimination, the suppliers of a market where this type of discrimination is exhibited are capable of differentiating between consumer classes. Examples of this differentiation are student or senior discounts. For example, a student or a senior consumer will have a different willingness to pay than an average consumer, where the reservation price is presumably lower because of budget constraints. Thus, the supplier sets a lower price for that consumer because the student or senior has a more elastic price elasticity of demand (see the discussion of price elasticity of demand as it applies to revenues from the first degree price discrimination, above). The supplier is once again capable of capturing more market surplus than would be possible without price discrimination.

Note that it is not always advantageous to the company to discriminate price even if it is possible, especially for second and third degree discrimination. In some circumstances, the demands of different classes of consumers will encourage suppliers to simply ignore one/some class(es) and target entirely to the other(s). Whether it is profitable to discriminate is determined price by the specifics of a particular market.

Third Degree (Multi-Market) Price Discrimination

This is the most frequently found form of price discrimination and involves charging different prices for the same product in different segments of the market. The key is that third degree discrimination is linked directly to consumers' willingness and ability to pay for goods or services. It means that the prices charged may bear little or no relation to the cost of production.

The market is usually separated in two ways: by time or by geography. For example, exporters may charge a higher price in overseas markets if demand is estimated to be more inelastic than it is in home markets. MC=AC

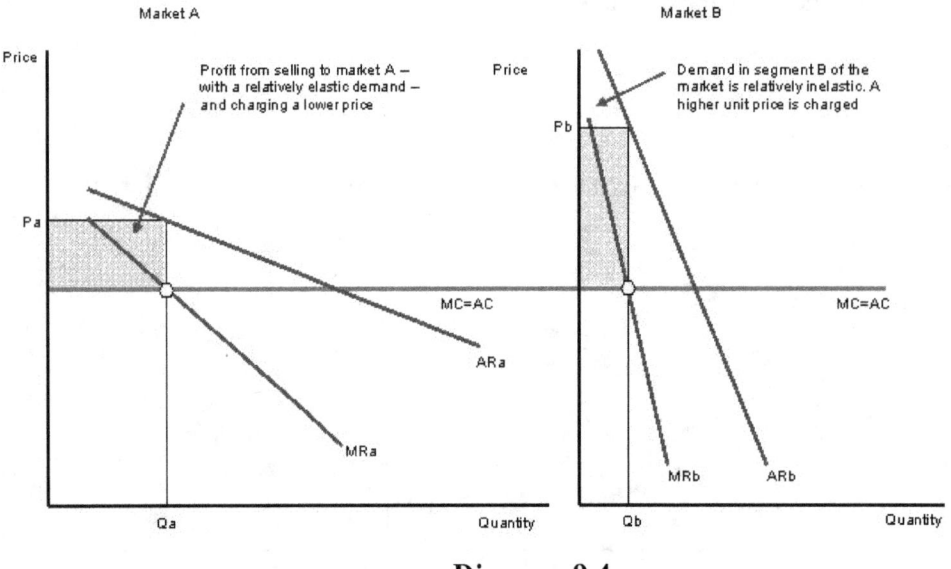

Diagram 9.4

Suppose a firm has separated a market by time into a peak market with inelastic demand, and an off-peak market with elastic demand. The demand and marginal revenue curves for the peak market and off peak markets are labelled A and B respectively. This is illustrated in the diagram above. Assuming a constant marginal cost for supplying to each group of consumers, the firm aims to charge a profit maximising price to each group.

In the peak market the firm will produce where MRa = MC and charge price Pa, and in the off-peak market the firm will produce where MRb = MC and charge price Pb. Consumers with an inelastic demand for the product will pay a higher price (Pa) than those with an elastic demand who will be charged Pb.

Price Skimming

In price skimming, price varies over time. Typically a company starts selling a new product at a relatively high price then gradually reduces the price as the low price elasticity segment gets satiated. Price skimming is closely related to the concept of yield management. Price skimming is a pricing strategy in which a marketer sets a relatively high price for a product or service at first, then lowers the price over time. It is a temporal version of price discrimination/yield management. It allows the firm to recover its sunk costs quickly before competition steps in and lowers the market price.

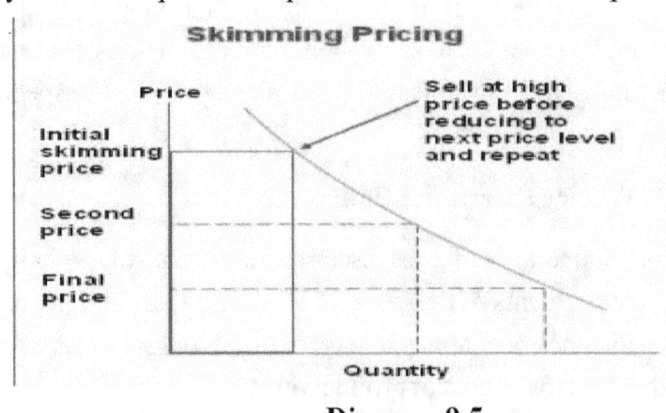

Diagram 9.5

108

Price skimming is sometimes referred to as riding down the demand curve. The objective of a price skimming strategy is to capture the consumer surplus. If this is done successfully, then theoretically no customer will pay less for the product than the maximum they are willing to pay. In practice, it is almost impossible for a firm to capture all of this surplus.

Combination

These types are not mutually exclusive. Thus a company may vary pricing by location, but then offer bulk discounts as well. Airlines use several different types of price discrimination, including:

- Bulk discounts to wholesalers, consolidators, and tour operators
- Incentive discounts for higher sales volumes to travel agents and corporate buyers
- Seasonal discounts, incentive discounts, and even general prices that vary by location. The price of a flight from say, Singapore to Beijing can vary widely if one buys the ticket in Singapore compared to Beijing (or New York or Tokyo or elsewhere). In online ticket sales this is achieved by using the customer's credit card billing address to determine his location.
- Discounted tickets requiring advance purchase and/or Saturday stays. Both restrictions have the effect of excluding business travelers, who typically travel during the workweek and arrange trips on shorter notice.
- First degree price discrimination based on customer. It is not accidental that hotel or car rental firms may quote higher prices to their loyalty program's top tier members than to the general public

9.5 International Price Discrimination: Dumping

In economics, "dumping" can refer to any kind of predatory pricing. However, the word is now generally used only in the context of international trade law, where dumping is defined as the act of a manufacturer in one country exporting a product to another country at a price which is either below the price it charges in its home market or is below its costs of production. The term has a negative connotation, but advocates of free markets see "dumping" as beneficial for consumers and believe that protectionism to prevent it would have net negative consequences. Advocates for workers and laborers however, believe that safeguarding businesses against predatory practices, such as dumping, help alleviate some of the harsher consequences of free trade between economies at different stages of development (see protectionism). The Bolkestein directive, for example, was accused in Europe of being a form of "social dumping," as it favored competition between workers, as exemplified by the Polish Plumber stereotype. While there are very few examples of a national scale dumping that succeeded in producing a national-level monopoly, there are several examples of dumping that produced a monopoly in regional markets for certain industries. Ron Chenow points to the example of regional oil monopolies in Titan : The Life of John D. Rockefeller, Sr. where Rockefeller receives a message from Colonel Thompson outlining an approved strategy where oil in one market, Cincinnati, would be sold at or below cost to drive competition's profits down and force them to exit the market. In another area where other independent businesses were already driven out, namely in Chicago, prices would be increased by a quarter.

A standard technical definition of dumping is the act of charging a lower price for a good in a foreign market than one charges for the same good in a domestic market. This is often referred to as selling at less than "fair value". Under the World Trade Organization (WTO) Agreement, dumping is condemned (but is not prohibited) if it causes or threatens to cause material injury to a domestic industry in the importing country.

Remedies and penalties

In the United States, domestic firms can file an antidumping petition under the regulations determined by the United States Department of Commerce, which determines "less than fair value" and the International Trade Commission, which determines "injury". These proceedings operate on a timetable governed by U.S. law. The Department of Commerce has regularly found that products have been sold at less than fair value in U.S. markets. If the domestic industry is able to establish that it is being injured by the dumping, then antidumping duties are imposed on goods imported from the dumpers' country at a percentage rate calculated to counteract the dumping margin.

Related to antidumping duties are "countervailing duties". The difference is that countervailing duties seek to offset injurious subsidization while antidumping duties offset injurious dumping.

Some commentators have noted that domestic protectionism, and lack of knowledge regarding foreign cost of production, lead to the unpredictable institutional process surrounding investigation. Members of the WTO can file complaints against anti-dumping measures.

Legal issues

If a company exports a product at a price lower than the price it normally charges on its own home market, it is said to be "dumping" the product. Opinions differ as to whether or not this is unfair competition, but many governments take action against dumping in order to defend their domestic industries. The WTO agreement does not pass judgment. Its focus is on how governments can or cannot react to dumping-it disciplines anti-dumping actions, and it is often called the "Anti-Dumping Agreement". (This focuses only on the reaction to dumping contrasts with the approach of the Subsidies & Countervailing Measures Agreement.)

The legal definitions are more precise, but broadly speaking the WTO agreement allows governments to act against dumping where there is genuine ("material") injury to the competing domestic industry. In order to do that the government has to be able to show that dumping is taking place, calculate the extent of dumping (how much lower the export price is compared to the exporter's home market price), and show that the dumping is causing injury or threatening to do so.

Definitions and degrees of dumping

While permitted by the WTO, General Agreement on Tariffs and Trade (GATT) (Article VI) allows countries the option of taking action against dumping. The Anti-Dumping Agreement clarifies and expands Article VI, and the two operate together. They allow countries to act in a way that would normally break the GATT principles of binding a tariff and not discriminating between trading partners-typically anti-dumping action means charging extra import duty on the particular product from the particular exporting country in order to bring its price closer to the "normal value" or to remove the injury to domestic industry in the importing country.

There are many different ways of calculating whether a particular product is being dumped heavily or only lightly. The agreement narrows down the range of possible options. It provides three methods to calculate a product's "normal value". The main one is based on the price in the exporter's domestic market. When this cannot be used, two alternatives are available-the price charged by the exporter in another country, or a calculation based on the combination of the exporter's production costs, other expenses and normal profit margins. And the agreement also specifies how a fair comparison can be made between the export price and what would be a normal price.

Calculating the extent of dumping on a product is not enough. Anti-dumping measures can only be applied if the dumping is hurting the industry in the importing country. Therefore, a detailed investigation has to be conducted according to specified rules first. The investigation must evaluate all relevant economic factors that have a bearing on the state of the industry in question. If the investigation shows dumping is taking place and domestic industry is being hurt, the exporting company can undertake to raise its price to an agreed level in order to avoid anti-dumping import duty.

Procedures in investigation and litigation

Detailed procedures are set out on how anti-dumping cases are to be initiated, how the investigations are to be conducted, and the conditions for ensuring that all interested parties are given an opportunity to present evidence. Anti-dumping measures must expire five years after the date of imposition, unless a review shows that ending the measure would lead to injury.

Anti-dumping investigations are to end immediately in cases where the authorities determine that the margin of dumping is, de minimis, or insignificantly small (defined as less than 2% of the export price of the product). Other conditions are also set. For example, the investigations also have to end if the volume of dumped imports is negligible (i.e., if the volume from one country is less than 3% of total imports of that product-although investigations can proceed if several countries, each supplying less than 3% of the imports, together account for 7% or more of total imports). The agreement says member countries must inform the Committee on Anti-Dumping Practices about all preliminary and final anti-dumping actions, promptly and in detail. They must also report on all investigations twice a year. When differences arise, members are encouraged to consult each other. They can also use the WTO's dispute settlement procedure.

9.6 Disadvantages of Price Discrimination

1. Some consumers will end up paying higher prices. These higher prices are likely to be allocatively inefficient because P>MC.
2. Decline in consumer surplus.
3. Those who pay higher prices may not be the poorest.
4. There may be administration costs in separating the markets.
5. Profits from price discrimination could be used to finance predatory pricing.

9.7 Price Discrimination-Harmful or Beneficial to Society

Pigou and Joan Robinson have analyzed the circumstances under which price discrimination is harmful or beneficial to society. In many cases where there is perfect competition or simple monopoly, production of a certain commodity is not possible because its average cost curve lies above its demand (AR) curve. But under price discrimination, the average cost curve is likely to be below the average revenue curve at some point. Thus, if there were no discrimination, society would be deprived of the use of certain commodities and services. As emphasized by Mrs Robinson: "It may happen, for instance, that a railway would not be built, or a country doctor would not set up practice, if discrimination were forbidden. From the point of view of society, it is only necessary that the concern should make sufficient profits to maintain the efficiency of the plant, and not a profit which would have been sufficient to justify the original investment." If a doctor charges a uniform fee from all his patients, his income may be so low as to induce him to leave his private practice and join some hospital. The community is thus deprived of his services in that particular area where he is practicing. If, however, he charges more fee from his rich patients than from the ordinary, his income is likely to be so high as to induce him from stay in that area.

Similarly, the existence of railways depends upon their charging higher rates to some customers than from others.

If discrimination occurs under conditions of falling average costs, it is actually beneficial to consumers because it results in larger output for the market. This is illustrated in Figure 4 where D is the average revenue curve of the discriminating monopolist and d/MR is the ordinary demand curve which becomes the MR curve to the discriminator. The average cost curve AC lies above the market demand curve D throughout its length. So no production is possible at any price on the D curve. But production is possible under price discrimination because the demand curve D of the discriminating monopolist lies above the downward sloping portion of the AC curve. Equilibrium is established at E where MC = MR and the output OQ is produced and sold at QP price and the discriminator earns RP profits per unit of output.

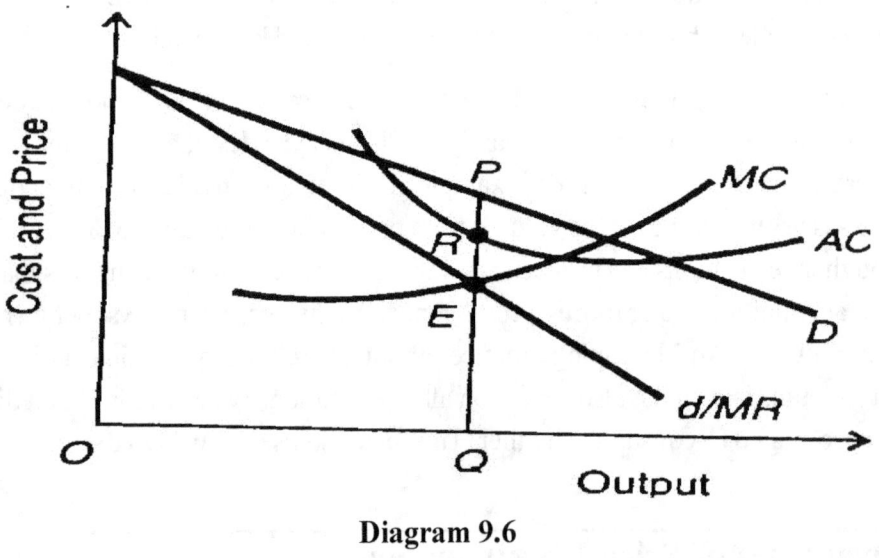

Diagram 9.6

Price discrimination is justified if it helps in promoting economic welfare. Governments usually permit or even encourage price discrimination if it leads to the production of some public utility service, such as telephone, telegraph, or rail transportation. In public utility services, the higher income groups are charged higher prices and the funds so collected may be used to subsidies the goods meant for the poor.

Price discrimination is also beneficial to society for it helps in reducing inequalities of personal incomes when higher prices or fees are charged from the rich than from the poor. In public utility services, the higher price charged from the higher income groups serves as a tool for income redistribution because the government may use these funds to subsidies the lower income groups. Thus price discrimination helps in promoting social welfare.

Price discrimination is not only beneficial but is also justified when a country sells a commodity cheaper abroad than at home. If a foreign market is elastic, more will be sold at a lower price. It means expansion in output, the use of larger resources of the economy, more employment and income to the community. Price discrimination of this type proves particularly useful if the industry obeys the law of decreasing costs. It implies the realization of larger economies of scale, lowering of costs and prices to the home market also. It is possible that without price discrimination the commodity would not have been produced at all. In that case, had it been imported from abroad, it would have cost the economy more both in monetary and real terms. Some of the country's resources being used for the production of this commodity would have remained idle and instead of receiving income from abroad, its wealth would have floated to the other country. May be, economies of scale could be realized only when the monopolist started producing for the foreign market. Hence price discrimination is justified.

Price discrimination is, however, harmful to society when it leads to a misdistribution of resources as between different uses with the result that output, employment and income are not maximized. Further, it may lead to the diversion of resources from their socially optimal uses. It leads to wastes of resources when people are made to pay higher prices for smaller quantities. Even on international plane when price discrimination takes the form of dumping, it deliberately shatters the economy of the other country by undercutting the foreign producers and forcing them to close their business. Such discrimination is highly undesirable.

9.8 Summary

Price discrimination is the practice of one retailer, wholesaler, or manufacturer charging different prices for the same items from different customer. This is a widespread practice. Price discrimination, as it is now understood, is separated into degrees. First, second and third degree price discrimination exist and apply to different pricing methods used by companies. Much depends on the understanding of the market in segments, and also the consumer's ability to pay a higher or lower price, called elasticity of demand. A person who might pay more for an item is thought to have a low elasticity of demand. Another person who will not pay as much has a high elasticity of demand.

9.9 Key Words

- **Price discrimination:** Price discrimination exists when sales of identical goods or services are transacted at different prices from the same provider. In general, the practice of charging different customers different prices is called price discrimination.

- **First degree price discrimination:** Price discrimination exists when sales of identical goods or services are transacted at different prices from the same provider. In general, the practice of charging different customers different prices is called price discrimination.

- **Second degree price discrimination:** Price discrimination exists when sales of identical goods or services are transacted at different prices from the same provider. In general, the practice of charging different customers different prices is called price discrimination.

- **Third degree price discrimination:** Price discrimination exists when sales of identical goods or services are transacted at different prices from the same provider. In general, the practice of charging different customers different prices is called price discrimination.

- **Dumping:** Selling goods abroad at a price below that charged in the domestic market.

9.10 Self Assessment Test

1   What is price discrimination? What are the conditions for discriminating price?

2   What are the objectives of price discrimination?

3   Briefly explain types of price discrimination.

4   What do you think price discrimination-harmful or beneficial to society?

5   What is international price discrimination? Explain its legal issues.

9.11 Suggested Books/References

1.   Mansfield E.C. : Micro Economics - Selected Reading W.W. Norten, New York

2.   Koutsoyiannis A: Reading in applied Economics: Oxford Clarendoor Press.

10 Pricing Strategies

Unit Structure

10.0 Objectives

After studying this unit, you should be able to understand:

- The concept of pricing strategy.
- Pricing strategies followed by firms in specific situations.
- Pricing strategy and their impact on demand.
- The objectives of pricing strategy.

10.1 Introduction

In every economics system, the prices of goods and services are crucial. A price is a sacrifice for one who pays it but it is a gain for one who gets it. Everybody is concerned with the prices in one way or another. The price of the commodity would be determined by the market itself through interplay of demand and supply for the commodity, because there is a relationship between price and quantity demanded, it is important to understand the impact of pricing on sales by estimating the demand curve for the product. For existing products, experiments can be performed at prices above and below the current price in order to determine the price elasticity of demand. Inelastic demand indicates that price increases might be feasible.

Pricing strategy las an instrument to achieve the objective of a firm and it should be formulated in such a way as to maximize the sales revenue and profit. Maximum profit refers to the highest possible profit. In the short run, a firm not only should be able to recover its total costs, but also should get excess revenue over costs.

One of the most difficult, yet important, issues you must decide as an entrepreneur is how much to charge for your product or service. While there is no one single right way to determine your pricing strategy, fortunately there are some guidelines that will help you with your decision.

10.2 Objectives of Pricing Strategy

The firm's pricing strategy objectives must be identified in order to determine the optimal pricing in different market situations. Common objectives include the following:

- Current profit maximization - seeks to maximize current profit, taking into account revenue and costs. Current profit maximization may not be the best objective if it results in lower long-term profits.

- Current revenue maximization - seeks to maximize current revenue with no regard to profit margins. The underlying objective often is to maximize long-term profits by increasing market share and lowering costs.

- Maximize quantity - seeks to maximize the number of units sold or the number of customers served in order to decrease long-term costs as predicted by the experience curve.

- Maximize profit margin - attempts to maximize the unit profit margin, recognizing that quantities will be low.

- Quality leadership - use price to signal high quality in an attempt to position the product as the quality leader.

- Partial cost recovery - an organization that has other revenue sources may seek only partial cost recovery.

- Survival - in situations such as market decline and overcapacity, the goal may be to select a price that will cover costs and permit the firm to remain in the market. In this case, survival may take a priority over profits, so this objective is considered temporary.

- Status quo - the firm may seek price stabilization in order to avoid price wars and maintain a moderate but stable level of profit.

10.3 Cost-Plus Pricing

Cost-plus pricing is also known as 'mark-up pricing', 'average cost pricing' or 'full cost pricing'. The cost-plus pricing is the most common method of pricing used by the manufacturing firms. It is used primarily because it is easy to calculate and requires little information. There are several varieties, but the common thread in all of them is you first calculate the cost of the product, and then include an additional amount to represent profit.

Calculating price using the cost-plus method

There are several ways of determining cost, and the profit can be added as either a percentage markup or an absolute amount. One example is:

$P = (AVC + FC\%) \times (1 + MK\%)$

Where:

- P = price
- AVC = average variable cost
- FC% = percentage allocation of fixed costs
- MK% = percentage markup

For example: If variable costs are 30 yen, the allocation to cover fixed costs is 10 yen, and you feel you need a 50% markup then you would charge a price of 60 yen:

$P = (30 + 10) \times (1 + 0.50)$

$P = 40 \times 1.5$

$P = 60$

An alternative way of doing the same calculation is:

$P = (AVC + FC\%) / (1 ? MK\%)$

To make things simpler, some firms, particularly retailers, ignore fixed costs and just use the purchase price paid to their suppliers as the cost term. They indirectly incorporate the fixed cost allocation into the markup percentage. To simplify things even further, sometimes a fixed amount is applied rather than a percentage. This fixed amount is usually determined by head-office to make it easy for franchisees and store managers. This is sometimes referred to as turnkey pricing.

Another variant of cost plus pricing is activity based pricing. This involves being more careful in determining costs. Instead of using arbitrary expense categories when allocating overhead, every activity is linked to the resources it uses.

Advantages of cost-plus pricing :-

1. easy to calculate
2. minimal information requirements
3. easy to administer
4. tends to stabilize markets - insulated from demand variations and competitive factors
5. ethical advantages

Disadvantages of cost-plus pricing :-

1. tends to ignore the role of consumers
2. tends to ignore the role of competitors
3. use of historical accounting costs rather than replacement value
4. inclusion of sunk costs rather than just using incremental costs
5. ignores opportunity costs

10.4 Pricing over Life-Cycle of a Product

Product life cycle management (or PLCM) is the succession of strategies used by business management as a product goes through its life cycle. The life-cycle of a product is generally divided into four stages: (i) Introduction (ii) Growth, (iii) Maturity, (iv) Decline. Diagram 11.1presents the four stages of a product's life-cycle through a curve showing the behavior of the total sales over the life cycle. The introduction phase is the period taken to introduce the product to the market. The total sale during this period is limited to the quantity put on the market for trial with considerable advertisement. The sales during this period remain almost constant. Growth is the stage, after a successful trail, during which the product gains popularity among the consumers and sales increase at an increasing rate as a result of cumulative effect of advertisement over the initial stage. Maturity is the stage in which sales continue to increase but at a lower rate and the total sale eventually becomes constant. After the maturity stage, comes the stage of decline in which total sales register a declining trend for such reasons as (i) increase in the availability of substitutes, and (ii) the loss of distinctiveness of the product.

116

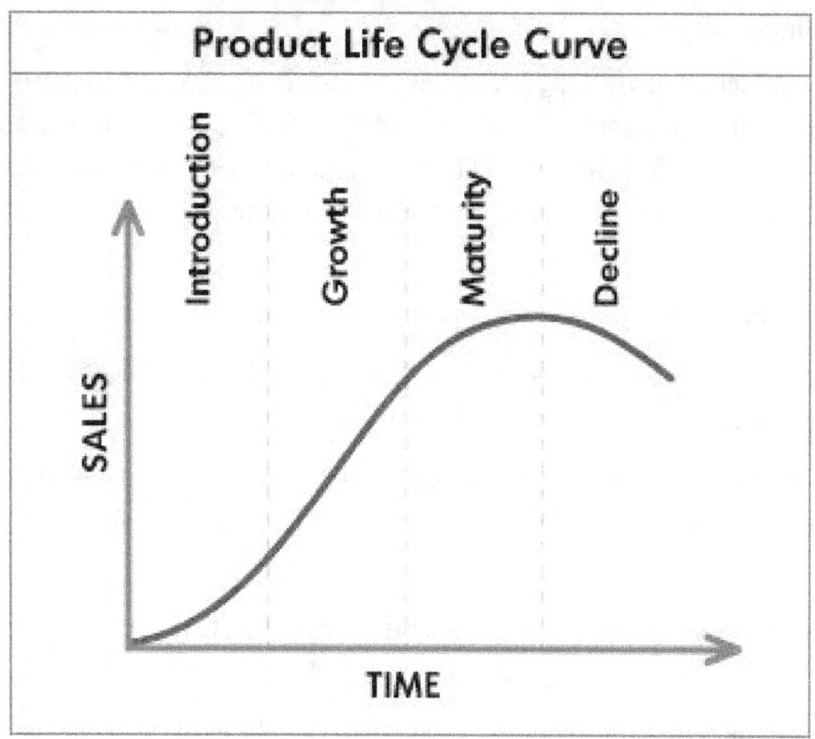

Diagram 10.1

The pricing strategy varies from stage to stage over the life-cycle of a product depending on the market conditions. From the pricing strategy point of view, growth and maturity stages may be treated likewise. We have first discussed the pricing of a product in its initial stage as pricing of a new product and then in the 'maturity' and 'decline' stage.

Pricing a New Product:

Pricing policy in respect of a new product depends on whether or not close substitutes are available. Depending on whether or not close substitutes are available, in pricing a new product, generally two kinds of pricing strategies are suggested, viz., (i) price skimming and (ii) price penetration.

Price Skimming:-

It is a pricing strategy in which a marketer sets a relatively high price for a product or service at first, then lowers the price over time. It is a temporal version of price discrimination/yield management. It allows the firm to recover its sunk costs quickly before competition steps in and lowers the market price.

Price skimming is sometimes referred to as riding down the demand curve. The objective of a price skimming strategy is to capture the consumer surplus. If this is done successfully, then theoretically no customer will pay less for the product than the maximum they are willing to pay. In practice, it is almost impossible for a firm to capture this entire surplus. The initial high price would generally be accompanied by heavy sales promoting expenditure. This policy succeeds for the following reasons.

First, in the initial stage of the introduction of product, demand is relatively inelastic because of consumers' desire for distinctiveness by the consumption of a new product.

Second, cross-elasticity is usually very low for lack of a close substitute.

Third, step-by-step skimming consumers' surplus available at the lower segments of demand curve.

117

Penetration Pricing:-

It is the pricing technique of setting a relatively low initial entry price, often lower than the eventual market price, to attract new customers. The strategy works on the expectation that customers will switch to the new brand because of the lower price. Penetration pricing is most commonly associated with a marketing objective of increasing market share or sales volume, rather than to make profit in the short term.

The success of penetration price policy requires the existence of the following conditions.

First, the short run demand for the product should have elasticity greater than unity. It helps in capturing the market at lower prices.

Second, economies of large-scale production are available to the firm with the increase in sales. Otherwise, increase in production would result in increase in costs which might reduce the competitiveness of the price.

Third, the product should have a high cross-elasticity in relation to rival products for the initial lower price to be effective.

Finally, the product, by nature should be such that it can be easily accepted and adopted by the consumers.

Pricing in Maturity Period:

Maturing period is the second stage in the life-cycle of a product. It is a stage between the growth period and decline period of sales. Sometimes maturity period is bracketed with saturation period. Maturity period may also be defined as the period of decline in the growth rate of sales (not the total sales) and the period of zero growth rate. The concept of maturity period is useful to the extent it gives out signals for taking precaution with regard to pricing policy. However, the concept itself does not provide guidelines for the pricing policy. Joel Dean suggests that the "first step for the manufacturer whose specialty is about to slip into the commodity category is to reduce real...prices as soon as the system of deterioration appears." But he warns that "this does not mean that the manufacturer should declare open price war in the industry". He should rather move in the direction of "product improvement and market segmentation".

Pricing a Product in Decline:

The product in decline is one that enters the post-maturity stage. In this stage, the total sale of the product starts declining. The first step in pricing strategy in this stage is obviously to reduce the price. The product should be reformulated and remodeled to suit the consumers' preferences. It is a common practice in the book trade. When the sale of a hard-bound edition reaches saturation, paper-back edition is brought into the market. This facility is, however, limited to only a few

10.5 Multiple Product Pricing

The price theory or microeconomic models of price determination are based on the assumption that a firm produces a single, homogeneous product. In actual practice, however, production of a single homogeneous product by a firm is an exception rather than a rule. Almost all firms have more than one product in their line of production. Even the most specialized firms produce a commodity in multiple models, styles and sizes, each so much differentiated from the other that each model or size of the product may be considered a different product. For example, the various models of refrigerators, TV sets, radio and car models produced by the same company may be treated as different products for at least pricing purpose. The various models are so differentiated that consumers view them as different products and in some cases, as perfect substitutes for each other. It is, therefore, not surprising that each model or product has different AR and MR curves and that one product of the firm competes against the other product. The pricing under these conditions is known as multi-product pricing or product-line pricing.

The major problem in pricing multiple products is that each product has a separate demand curve. But, since all of them are produced under one organization by interchangeable production facilities, they have only one inseparable marginal, cost curve. That is, while revenue curves, AR and MR, are separate for each product, cost curves, AC and MC, are inseparable. Therefore, the marginal rule of pricing cannot be applied straightaway to fix the price of each product separately. The problem, however, has been provided with a solution by E.W. Clements. The solution is similar to the one employed to illustrate third degree price discrimination. As a discriminating monopoly tries to maximize its revenue in all its markets, so does a multi-product firm in respect of each of its products.

To illustrate the multiple product pricing, let us suppose that a firm has four different products - A, B, C and D in its line of production. The AR and MR curves for the four goods are shown in four segments of Diagram 10.2 The marginal cost for all the products taken together is shown by

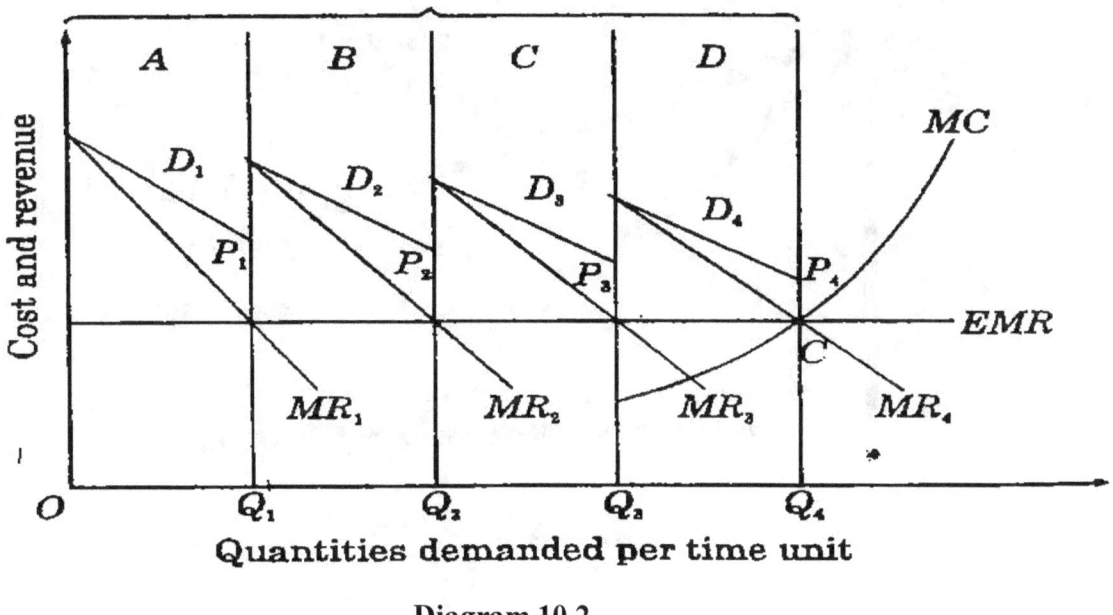

Diagram 10.2

The marginal cost for all the products taken together is shown by the curve MC, which is the factory marginal cost curve. Let us suppose that when the MRs for the individual products are horizontally summed up, the aggregate MR (not given in the figure) passes through point C on the MC curve. If a line parallel to the X-axis, is drawn from point C to the Y-axis through the MRs, the intersecting points will show the points where MC and MRs are equal for each product, as shown by the line EMR, the Equal Marginal Revenue line. The points of intersection between EMR and MRs determine the output level and price for each product. The output of the four products are given as OQ1 of product A; Q1Q2 of B; Q2Q3 of C; Q3Q4 of D. The respective prices for the four products are: P1Q1 for product A; P2Q2 for B; P3Q3 for C, and P4Q4 for D. These price and output combinations maximize the profit from each product and hence the overall profit of the firm.

119

Transfer pricing refers to the setting, analysis, documentation, and adjustment of charges made between related parties for good, services, or use of property (including intangible property). Transfer prices among components of an enterprise may be used to reflect allocation of resources among such components, or for other purposes. we can say the price at which transfer takes place called transfer price. A high price will increase profits of the units at the earlier stage of production, whereas a low price will make later stage production more profitable. while an incorrect price can affect the total profit earned by the firm.

Transfer Pricing with No External Market

The discussion in this section explains an economic theory behind optimal transfer pricing with optimal defined as transfer pricing that maximizes overall firm profits in a non-realistic world with no taxes, no capital risk, no development risk, no externalities or any other frictions which exist in the real world. In practice a great many factors influence the transfer prices that are used by multinational corporations, including performance measurement, capabilities of accounting systems, import quotas, customs duties, VAT, taxes on profits, and (in many cases) simple lack of attention to the pricing.

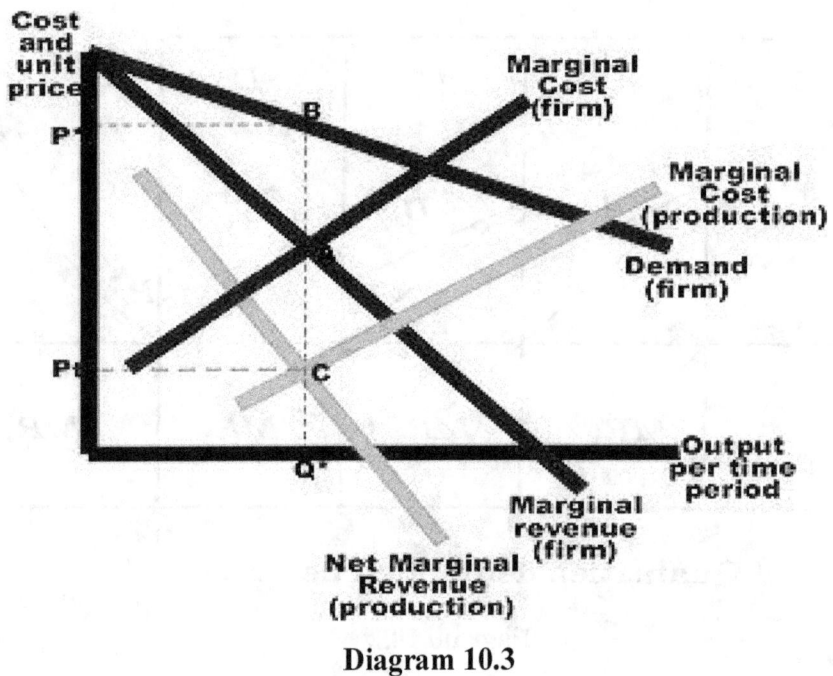

Diagram 10.3

From marginal price determination theory, the optimum level of output is that where marginal cost equals marginal revenue. That is to say, a firm should expand its output as long as the marginal revenue from additional sales is greater than their marginal costs. In the diagram that follows, this intersection is represented by point A, which will yield a price of P*, given the demand at point B.

It can be shown algebraically that the intersection of the firm's marginal cost curve and marginal revenue curve (point A) must occur at the same quantity as the intersection of the production division's marginal cost curve with the net marginal revenue from production (point C).

Transfer Pricing with a Competitive External Market

When a firm is selling some of its product to itself, and only to itself (i.e. there is no external market for that particular transfer good), then the picture gets more complicated, but the outcome remains the same. The demand curve remains the same. The optimum price and quantity remain the same. But marginal cost of production can be separated from the firm's total marginal costs. Likewise, the marginal revenue associated with the production division can be separated from the marginal revenue for the total firm. This is referred to as the Net Marginal Revenue in production (NMR) and is calculated as the marginal revenue from the firm minus the marginal costs of distribution.

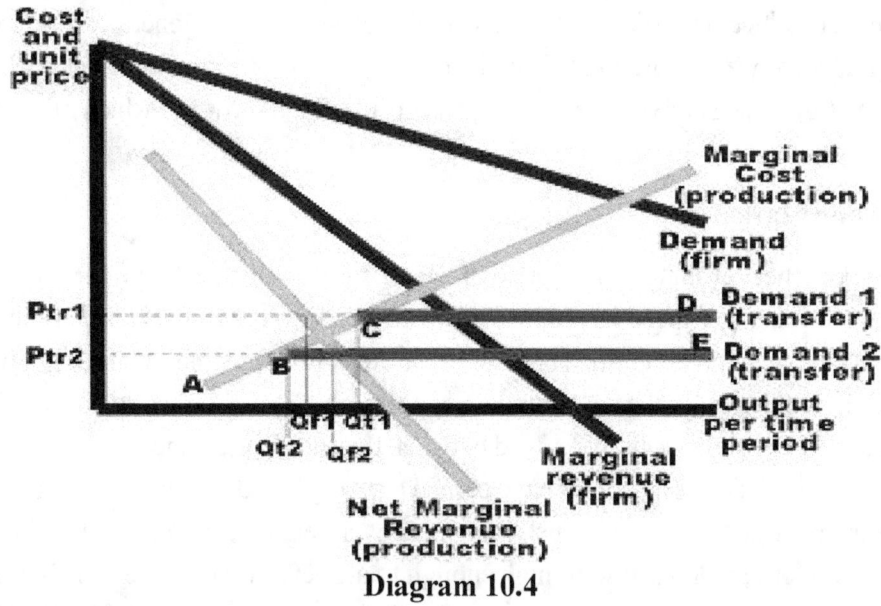

Diagram 10.4

If the production division is able to sell the transfer good in a competitive market (as well as internally), then again both must operate where their marginal costs equal their marginal revenue, for profit maximization. Because the external market is competitive, the firm is a price taker and must accept the transfer price determined by market forces (their marginal revenue from transfer and demand for transfer products becomes the transfer price). If the market price is relatively high (as in Ptr1 in the next diagram), then the firm will experience an internal surplus (excess internal supply) equal to the amount Qt1 minus Qf1. The actual marginal cost curve is defined by points A,C,D.

Transfer Pricing with an Imperfect External Market

If the firm is able to sell its transfer goods in an imperfect market, then it need not be a price taker. There are two markets each with its own price (Pf and Pt in the next diagram).

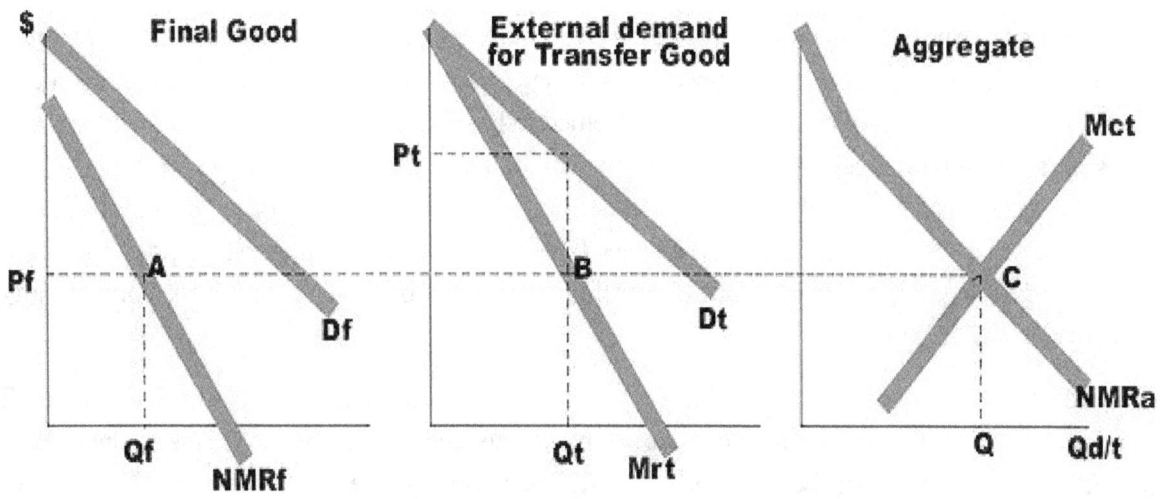

Diagram 10.5

121

The aggregate market is constructed from the first two. That is, point C is a horizontal summation of points A and B (and likewise for all other points on the Net Marginal Revenue curve (NMRa)). The total optimum quantity (Q) is the sum of Qf plus Qt.

10.7 Pricing for Established Products

In pricing a product in relation to its well established substitutes, generally three types of pricing strategies are adopted, viz., (i) pricing below the ongoing price, (ii) pricing at par with the prevailing market price, and (iii) pricing above the existing market price. Let us now see which of these strategies are adopted under what conditions.

Pricing Below the Market-Price:

Pricing below the prevailing market price of the substitutes is generally preferred under two conditions. First, if a firm wants to expand its product-mix with a view to utilizing its unused capacity in the face of tough competition with the established brands, the strategy of pricing below the market price is generally adopted. This strategy gives the new brand an opportunity to gain popularity and establish itself. For this, however, a high cross-elasticity of demand between the substitute brands is necessary. This strategy may, however, not work if existing brands have earned a strong brand loyalty of the consumers. If so, the price incentive from the new producers must, therefore, overweigh the brand loyalty of the consumers of the established products, and must also be high enough to attract new consumers. This strategy is similar to the penetrating pricing. Second, this technique has been found to be more successful in the case of innovative products. When the innovative product gains popularity, the price may be gradually raised to the level of market price.

Pricing at Market Price:

Pricing at par with the market price of the existing brands is considered to be the most reasonable pricing strategy for a product which is being sold in a strongly competitive market. In such a market, keeping the price below the market price is not of much avail because the product can be sold in any quantity at the existing market rate. The strategy is also adopted when the seller is not a 'price leader'. It is rather a 'price-taker' in an oligopolistic market. This is, in fact, a very common pricing strategy, rather the most common practice.

Pricing Above the Existing Market-Price:

The strategy is adopted when a seller intends to achieve a prestigious position among the sellers in the locality. This is a more common practice in case of products considered to be a commodity of conspicuous consumption of prestige goods of deemed to be of much superior quality. Consumers of such goods prefer shopping in a gorgeous shop of a posh locality of the city. This is known as the 'Veblen Effect'. Sellers of such goods rely on their customers' high propensity to consume a prestigious commodity. After the seller achieves the distinction of selling high quality goods, though at a high price, they may sell even the ordinary goods at a price much higher than the market price. This practice is common among sellers of readymade garments.

Besides, a firm may sets a high price for its product if it pursues the 'skimming price strategy'. This pricing strategy is more suitable for innovative products when the firm can be sure of the distinctiveness of its product. The demand for the commodity must have a low cross-elasticity in respect of competing goods.

10.8 Peak-load Pricing

In this pricing technique applied to public goods. Instead of different demands for the same public good, we consider the demands for a public good in different periods of the day, month or year, then finding the optimal capacity (quantity supplied) and, afterwards, the optimal peak-load prices.

This has particular applications in public goods such as public urban transportation, where day demand (peak period) is usually much higher than night demand (off-peak period). By subtracting the marginal costs of operation from the original demands we find the marginal benefits of capacity, which must then be vertically aggregated and equated to the marginal cost of increasing capacity. With the optimal capacity found, the optimal peak-load prices are found by adding the marginal costs of operation to the marginal benefit generated, in each period, by the optimal capacity. It may happen, however, that the optimal capacity is not fully used during the off-peak period. In that case, the capacity expansion will be totally supported by the peak demanders.

As Diagram 10.6 shows, if electricity price is fixed in accordance with peak-load demand OP3 will be the price and if it is fixed according to off-load demand, price will be OP1. The problem is what price should be fixed? If a 'peak-load' price (OP3) is charged uniformly in all reasons, it will be unfair because consumers will be charged for what they do not consume. Besides, it may affect business activities adversely. If electricity production is a public monopoly, the government will not allow a uniform 'peak-load' price.

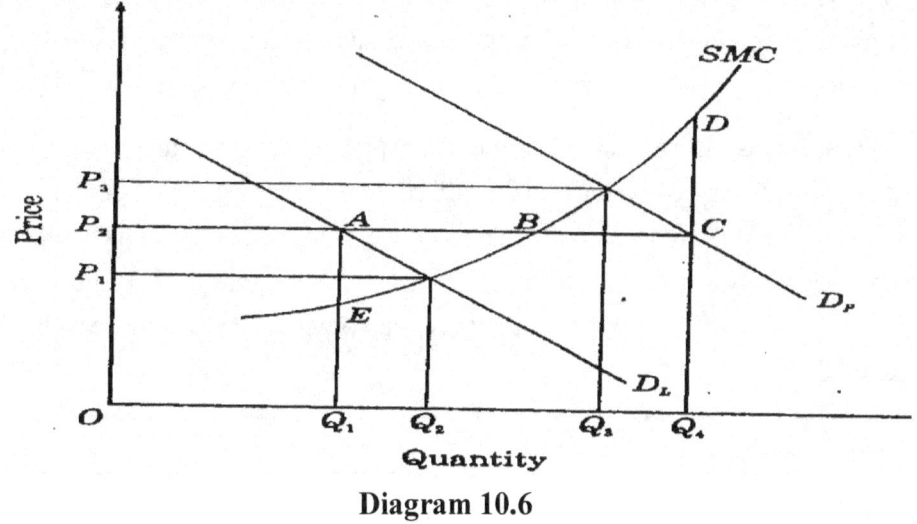

Diagram 10.6

On the other hand, if a uniform 'off load' price (OP1) is charged, production will fall to OQ2 and there will be acute shortage of electricity during peak hours. It leads to 'breakdowns' and 'load-shedding' during peak-load periods, which disrupt production and make life miserable. This is a regular feature in Delhi, the capital city of India. This is because electricity rates in Delhi are said to be one of the lowest in the country.

Alternatively, if an average of the two prices, say P2 is charged, it will have the demerits of both 'peak-load' and 'off-load' prices. There will be an excess production to the extend of AB during the 'off-load' period, which will go waste as it cannot be stored. It production is restricted to OQ1, price P2 will be unfair. And, during the 'peak-load' period, there will be a shortage to the extent of BC, which can be produced only at an extra marginal cost of CD.

123

10.9 Ramsey Pricing

If an enterprise has common costs, marginal cost pricing may not be feasible. Ramsey pricing is the second best alternative that allows the firm to recover its cost while minimizing adverse effects of allocative efficiency.It is applicable to public utilities or regulation of natural monopolies, such as telecom firms.

Ramsey pricing is sometimes consistent with a government's objectives because Ramsey pricing is economically efficient in the sense that it can maximize welfare under certain circumstances. There are, however, problems with Ramsey pricing. A profit-maximizing operator will choose Ramsey prices only if all markets are equally monopolistic or equally competitive. If markets are not equally monopolistic or competitive, then the regulator has an interest in taking steps to ensure that the extent to which the operator can use Ramsey pricing is limited to groups of services that are subject to similar degrees of competition. Regulators typically do this by forming baskets of services that are subject to similar degrees of competition and allowing the operator price flexibility within each service basket. Even though Ramsey pricing can be economically efficient, it may not be consistent with the government's goal of providing affordable service to the poor and the rate by which prices change to achieve Ramsey-efficient prices may not be consistent with political sustainability. As a result of these two concerns, the regulator sometimes limits the operator's ability to pursue Ramsey pricing within a service basket. In the case of services to the poor, the regulator may place upper limits on the prices. Lastly, regulators often note that Ramsey pricing is a form of price discrimination - although not necessarily a bad form of price discrimination - and customers sometimes object to it on that basis. The public sometimes believes that it is unfair to cause one type of customer to pay a higher mark-up above marginal cost than another type of customer. In such situations regulators may further limit an operator's ability to adopt Ramsey prices.

Practical issues exist with attempts to use Ramsey pricing for setting utility prices. It may be difficult to obtain data on different price elasticities for different customer groups. Also, some customers with relatively inelastic demands may acquire a strong incentive to seek alternatives if charged higher markups, thus undermining the approach. Politically speaking, customers with relatively inelastic demands may also be viewed as those for whom the service is more necessary or vital; charging those higher markups can be challenged as unfair.

10.10 Limit Pricing

A limit price is the price set by a monopolist to discourage economic entry into a market, and is illegal in many countries. The limit price is the price that the entrant would face upon entering as long as the incumbent firm did not decrease output. The limit price is often lower than the average cost of production or just low enough to make entering not profitable. The quantity produced by the incumbent firm to act as a deterrent to entry is usually larger than would be optimal for a monopolist, but might still produce higher economic profits than would be earned under perfect competition. The problem with limit pricing as strategic behavior is that once the entrant has entered the market, the quantity used as a threat to deter entry is no longer the incumbent firm's best response. This means that for limit pricing to be an effective deterrent to entry, the threat must in some way be made credible. A way to achieve this is for the incumbent firm to constrain itself to produce a certain quantity whether entry occurs or not. An example of this would be if the firm signed a union contract to employ a certain (high) level of labor for a long period of time.

10.11 Loss leader Pricing

A company loses money on one service but earns on a related product. This strategy is often implemented as a part of a promotion campaign. The intent of this practice is not only to have the customer buy the (loss leader) sale item, but other products that are not discounted. These bargains will attract customers who may then purchase other products/services even if they don't buy the product which price had been initially reduced. This is where a company will make up for the loss as it will be selling other items that generate high profits. One example is HP inkjet printers that are often sold to retail customers below their true value, at a price which seems to be affordable to most consumers. Moreover, these printers are sometimes offered for free - free after rebate, free with a purchase of an HP computer, etc. However, consumers have to pay the regular price for ink cartridges. It is ink cartridges, not the printers that generate high profits for the HP. Another example is Gillette's safety razor handles that are sold at a loss, but sales of disposable razor blades are very profitable.

Major forces influencing pricing are company's strategic goals, demand for its products or services, and/or competition. Management should pay particular attention when deciding on pricing methods since the success of the entire business depends on it.

10.12 Summary

Pricing decisions require a synthesis of economic and marketing principles, an appreciation of legal and ethical constraints, and the ability to use accounting, financial, and market research data. Pricers face different market conditions which require distinguished pricing strategies. One of the most important drivers of the variability on those conditions is the state of demand. In real business world, firms practices numerous pricing strategies followed by firms in specific situations.

10.13 Key Words

- **Cost-plus pricing:** Cost-plus pricing is the simplest pricing method. The firm calculates the cost of producing the product and adds on a percentage (profit) to that price to give the selling price.

- **Skimming:** Selling a product at a high price.

- **Penetration pricing:** Selling a product at a high price.

- **Limit price:** Limit price is the price that the entrant would face upon entering as long as the in cumbent firm did not decrease output.

- **Transfer pricing:** The price that is assumed to have been charged by one part of a company for products and services it provides to another part of the same company, in order to calculate each division's profit and loss separately.

- **Loss leader pricing:** A loss leader or leader is a product sold at a low price (at cost or below cost) to stimulate other, profitable sales.

- **Peak-load pricing:** it is a pricing technique applied to public goods Instead of different demands for the same public good, we consider the demands for a public good in different periods of the day, month or year, then finding the optimal capacity (quantity supplied) and, after wards, the optimal peak-load prices.

- **Ramsey pricing:** Ramsey pricing is concerned with prices that maximize the sum of industry consumer surplus and profits.

10.14 Self Assessment Test

1   What is transfer pricing? How is transfer price determined in the cases i) Transfer Pricing with No External Market ii) Transfer Pricing with a Competitive External Market iii) Transfer Pricing with an Imperfect External Market.

2   Differentiate between skimming price and penetration price policy. Which of these policies is relevant in pricing a new product under different competitive conditions in market?

3   Explain the objectives of pricing strategy.

4   Describe cost plus pricing.

5   What kind of pricing strategy is adopted over the life cycle of a product. what do you think will be an appropriate price policy when the demand reaches its saturation and substitute product are likely to enter the market?

6   Briefly explain the concept of Ramsey pricing

10.15 Suggested Books/Reference

1.   Mathur N.D.: Managerial Economics, Shivam Book House (P.) Limited, Jaipur

2.   Piny C.K., R.S. and D.L. Rulinfeld, Micro Economics, Prentice Hall, New Jersey